THE [illegible]OK OF JAMS AND PRESERVES

PAT HESKETH

WI BOOKS

First Published 1998 by WI Books

in association with Stable Ltd
Glebe House, Church Street,
Crediton, Devon EX17 2AF

Illustrated by Michael Lye and others

British Library Cataloguing in Publication Data.
A CIP catalogue record for this book is available from the British Library.

ISBN 0 947990 47 X

Printed and bound in Great Britain by Short Run Press Ltd, Exeter, Devon

Acknowledgements

WI Books and the Author are grateful to **Margaret Hanford** and **Dilwen Phillips** for their work on this revised edition of the author's original title, *The WI Book of Jams & Preserves,* in which many of these recipes first appeared.

WI Books and the Author also wish to thank **The Silver Spoon Company** for their support for this publication.

Note
Tests carried out at the Home Preservation section of the Long Ashton Research Station, Bristol, and with WI Markets, in conjunction with Tony D'Angeli in 1992 prove that the eating and keeping quality of preserves is the same when using beet and cane sugar.

CONTENTS

INTRODUCTION

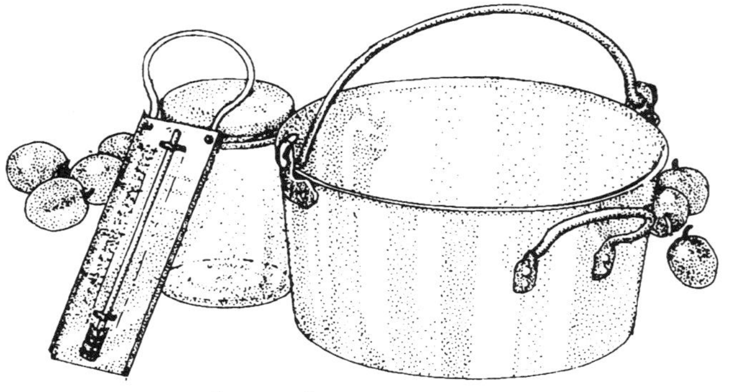

Sugar thermometer
and preserving pan

Foods have been preserved by many methods over the centuries, but in particular by drying, salting and freezing. Traditionally this has enabled housewives to provide a varied menu throughout the year. Modern growing methods and air freight have meant that most fruits and vegetables are always available in the supermarkets, but when locally grown fruits and vegetables are at their peak they are relatively cheap to purchase, and great personal satisfaction can be achieved from the making of preserves, and from seeing a larder containing a good selection of home-produced preserves.

Three types of preserves are relatively easy and cheap to make, and are eaten by most families: jams, marmalades and, to a lesser extent, some vinegar preserves such as chutneys.

To ensure that fruits and vegetables keep well when preserved, it is necessary to understand a little about enzyme action and about the control of spoilage organisms – yeasts, moulds and bacteria.

Enzymes

The action of enzymes brings about the natural ripening of fruits and also, given time, their decay. So it is necessary to stop enzyme action when fruits are ripe. This can be done by heat, as when making jams and bottling fruit.

Yeasts, moulds and bacteria

These are micro-organisms which can be killed by high temperatures and also have their growth inhibited by high concentrations of sugar and high acid content. Methods of making preserves take these principles into account.

Jams, jellies and marmalades should have a sufficiently high sugar content to prevent fermentation, but they must also, after making, be covered in a manner which prevents the re-entry of airborne micro-organisms (page 13).

Vinegar preserves should have a sufficiently high acid content to prevent the action of micro-organisms, and they should also be covered in a manner that prevents the vinegar from evaporating (page 51). The type of vinegar to use is stated in the introduction to VINEGAR PRESERVES (page 51). If in doubt, use malt vinegar unless it is a very pale coloured preserve or pickle, when a white, distilled vinegar is preferable.

1. EQUIPMENT

Preserves need very little special equipment and can be made quite satisfactorily with the equipment found in most kitchens. Here is a check-list:

- preserving pan (a pan with sloping sides)
- mixing bowl
- small basin
- plates
- colander
- sieve (nylon)
- small vegetable knife
- large chopping knife
- chopping board
- thermometer
- scales
- measuring jug
- measuring spoons
- large wooden spoons (preferably long-handled preserving spoon)
- tablespoon
- vegetable parer
- mincer
- juice extractor

Further equipment which may be useful:

- Juicer
- liquidiser/food processor
- slow cooker
- microwave oven
- pressure cooker

Preserves in the pressure cooker

A pressure cooker can be used to make preserves. Cooking time of the fruit for jam and marmalade, and fruit and vegetables, is greatly reduced. Always follow the manufacturer's instructions when using a pressure cooker.

Preserves in the microwave

Microwave ovens are particularly useful for making small batches of preserves. Jams, marmalades and chutneys can all be cooked in a microwave oven. They require less time and less attention than when cooked conventionally. It is recommended that the advice in the instruction book for each microwave oven be followed, but many of the recipes in this book can be made successfully using a microwave oven, providing it is remembered that only small quantities may be cooked at any time.

2. MEASUREMENTS

(a) All spoon measures are level unless otherwise stated.

3 tsp = 1 tbsp
8 tbsp = 1/4 pint = 5 fl oz = 150 ml

(b) All eggs used are medium size.

(c) **Use either the metric measures or the imperial in the recipes; do not mix them. They are not always equivalent to one another, because they have been tested and balanced separately.**

(d) All can sizes are approximate.

(e) All weights referred to in lists of ingredients for fruit, vegetables, etc., are unprepared weights unless stated otherwise.

3. PRESENTATION OF PRESERVES FOR SHOWING

(a) The schedule
When entering a competition or show, it is necessary to read the schedule carefully so that the rules and instructions are fully understood.

(b) Judge's marking
It may help competitors to know that although only one mark out of 20 is given for the appearance of the container – that is, the cover, cleanliness of the jar and the label – if the cover is not suitable for the preserve and will not keep it in good condition, the judge may not judge the preserve at all.

(c) The container
This must be suitable for the preserve and it must have the appropriate cover (see pages 13, 51, 71 for further details). The jar should be well filled, and the glass can be polished with methylated spirits to remove fingerprints. For carrying to the show, place the jar in a polythene bag and wrap it in either kitchen paper or corrugated card and pack it in a box.

(d) Label

The label must be straight and should be parallel to the bottom of the jar and placed as low as possible without wrinkling. The label should state: type of fruit, eg. raspberry; type of preserve, eg. jam; date of making, eg. 3rd July 1997. If frozen fruit has been used, this should be stated, and also the date of making, eg.:

Raspberry Jam
(frozen fruit)
10th January 1997

For bottled fruit the label should state the strength of the syrup or the usage to which the fruit may be put, eg.:

Bottled Gooseberries
(light syrup)
30th June 1997

Bottled Gooseberries
(for pies)
30th June 1997

The label on chutneys should state whether they are mild or hot.

(e) Colour

The colour should be good, and appropriate to the fruit the preserve was made from. In jams, jellies and marmalades the colour should be bright, even and sparkling. A dullness and slight darkening indicates overboiling of the preserve after the sugar was added. In chutneys, although the colour will be darkish, it should be bright, not muddy-looking.

(f) A full jar

The jar should be full – a low quantity in jams means that the cover is not able to do its job properly and that moulds may develop. A low quantity in chutney may indicate shrinkage which is caused by evaporation of the vinegar due to an incorrect cover.

(g) Consistency

The consistency of jams should show a good gel, and if whole fruits are present, as with blackcurrants, or peel shreds as in marmalade, these should be soft. Check that they are before adding the sugar. In chutneys, if there is 'free' vinegar floating on top of the preserves, this indicates that the chutney was insufficiently cooked before potting.

(h) Flavour

The flavour should be characteristic of the fruit, not spoilt by the use of inferior quality fruit, nor by overboiling or burning on the base of the pan.

For further information, refer to *On With the Show*, another WI Books publication. Check your local produce show schedule; there may be a class for preserves.

4. INGREDIENTS IN PRESERVATION

(a) Sugar

- *Cane and beet sugar* are both suitable for preservation. There is no difference in keeping quality.
- *Granulated sugar* is suitable for jam making.
- *Preserving sugar* (large crystal sugar) produces less scum than finer sugar.
- *Demerara or Brown sugar* add colour and flavour to preserves.
- *Jam sugar* contains natural pectin and citric acid to aid setting in fruits with low pectin content. It should not be used in preservation with other sugar, otherwise preserves will burn.

(b) Vinegar

- *Malt distilled vinegar,* an all-purpose vinegar.
- *Wine vinegar* is made from red or white wine; ideal for delicate preserves, eg. spiced fruits.
- *Cider vinegar* is made from apples.

  Wine and cider vinegars are sharper; they have a higher acid content than distilled vinegar.

(c) Salt

- *Table salt,* use only for flavouring; contains anti-caking ingredients and can cause clouding in preserves.
- *Cooking salt*, an all-purpose salt.
- *Sea salt* is purer salt than table salt.

5. TERMS USED IN PRESERVATION

Blanch	to boil briefly to loosen the skin of fruit.
Boil	when a liquid boils, the surface bubbles; *'rolling boil'* is the term used to describe sugar preserves when the liquid has risen in the pan and the surface bubbles.
Brine	salt and water solution used in pickling and preserving.
Pare	to peel thinly the zest from citrus fruits using a vegetable peeler or sharp knife.
Peel	the skin of citrus fruits, ie. the zest and pith.
Simmer	to cook in a liquid just below boiling point.
Zest	coloured oily outer skin of citrus fruit, used for flavouring.

JAMS & CONSERVES

In this chapter are some of the more traditional jam recipes using unusual fruits. If you like preserves with whole fruit in them, you will find here recipes for conserves, but remember that these will not set as well as jam does.

A good jam should:

- keep well;
- be clear and bright;
- be characteristic in colour;
- be well set, but not too stiff;
- have a distinct fruity flavour.

1. GETTING JAM TO SET WELL

Jam is a mixture of fruit and sugar cooked together to form a gel. To obtain a good gel (set), acid, pectin and sugar should be present in the correct proportions. Fruits vary in their acid content and the amount of fruit used when making jam varies according to whether or not it is rich in pectin. Extra acid is often added to fruit to help release the pectin present. If frozen fruit is used, increase the amount of fruit in the recipe by 10%.

(a) Pectin

Fruit with good pectin content

Black and Redcurrants
Cooking Apples
Crab Apples
Damsons
Gooseberries
some Plums
Quince

Fruit with medium pectin content

Early Blackberries
Fresh Apricots
Greengages
Loganberries
Raspberries

Fruit with poor pectin content

Late Blackberries
Cherries
Elderberries
Marrows
Tangerines
Pears
Rhubarb
Strawberries

Pectin Test

A test for *pectin* should be carried out after initial cooking of fruit with water.

1. Take 5 ml (1 tsp) juice, place it in a small glass. Cool.
2. Add 15 ml (3 tsp) methylated spirits.
3. Shake gently together.

(i) If a well-formed jelly-like clot is apparent, this shows a good pectin content.
(ii) If several small clots appear, this shows a medium pectin content.
(iii) If no clot appears, then no pectin is present.

If, after further cooking, still no recognisable clot appears, the addition of extra pectin will be necessary. This may be either juice from pectin-rich fruits, or commercial pectin. Use 50–100 ml per 450 g (2–4 fl oz per 1 lb) of fruit, or use jam sugar.

Very little or no pectin content — Medium pectin content — Good pectin content

(b) Acid

Helps to give a bright colour and prevents crystallization. It must be added at the beginning of cooking to fruits low in acid and to any vegetable jam, in the following proportions:

To 1.8 kg (4 lb) fruit:
30 ml (2 tbsp) lemon juice (1 average lemon)
or 5 ml (1/2 level tsp) citric acid or tartaric acid
or 150 ml (1/4 pint) redcurrant or gooseberry juice.

(c) Sugar

Granulated or preserving sugar may be used, but it must be thoroughly dissolved before the jam is brought to the boil. Many recipes are based on 60% sugar content, therefore if 2.7 kg (6 lb) sugar is used, a 4.5 kg (10 lb) yield could be expected.

(d) Fruit

Fruit should be dry, clean and fresh, and preferably slightly under-ripe.

2. STAGES IN JAM-MAKING

1. Initial cooking of fruit either on its own (eg. strawberries) or with water, or acid (ie. lemon juice). Fruit should *simmer* gently to break down the cell walls to release the pectin.

2. Carrying out the pectin test. A good result means that the cooking time with the sugar will not be prolonged and therefore the finished jam will have a good colour.

3. Addition of sugar, off the heat, then over a low heat, stirring to ensure that it is completely dissolved.

4. Returning pan to the heat, bringing to the boil, and boiling rapidly until setting point is reached.

5. Putting into clean jars and covering immediately with either a wax circle or metal twist. Jars should be filled to within 3 mm ($^{1}/_{8}$ inch) of the rim. A cover should be placed on each jar as it is filled.

6. Stone fruits can be stoned before cooking and stones placed in a muslin bag and simmered with the fruit to add flavour, or some stones can be cracked (using a weight or nutcrackers), the kernels should be blanched, then added to the fruit.

Note. The cellophane dust-covers used in conjunction with wax circles may be dampened on the upper-side and placed over the jar when either hot or cold, but never when warm.

Tests for setting point

(a) *Saucer test* (also known as plate, or wrinkle test). Have a plate cooling in the refrigerator. Place 5 ml (1 small tsp) jam on the plate and return to the refrigerator to cool for one minute. If the surface wrinkles as the finger is pushed through the jam, the jam has reached setting point. *(See note on next page.)*

It is important to keep the jam pan away from the heat during the test, otherwise the jam may go beyond setting point.

(b) *Flake test.* Dip the spoon into the boiling jam. Holding the spoon above the pan, twist it horizontally to cool the jam on the surface. Allow the jam to drop from the surface. If it has reached setting point, the jam will run together and form a flake on the edge of the spoon before breaking off cleanly.

(c) *Temperature test.* Place a sugar thermometer into the jam. Boil the jam until it reaches a temperature of 105°C (220°F). Have a pan of water at boiling point and keep the sugar thermometer in this when not in the jam pan.

Labelling
Clean the jars and label with details of contents and date of making (page 9).

Storage
All jams are best stored in cool, dry, dark, well ventilated places. Storage is a problem in centrally heated homes. Therefore jars with metal twist tops are recommended, because when properly used these form an airtight seal.

Conserves
A conserve is very similar to a jam in its making but the result is different in that the set is much softer and some fruits remain whole in a thick syrup.

APPLE AND DAMSON JAM

Yield 2.5 kg (5 lb)

1 kg (2 lb) cooking apples
1 kg (2 lb) damsons
450 ml (3/4 pint) water
1.5 kg (3 lb) sugar

1. Wash, peel, core and chop the apples. Wash the damsons.
2. Put the fruit in a preserving pan with the water, bring to the boil, reduce the heat and simmer until fruit is tender.
3. As the fruit cooks, the damson stones should rise to the surface; remove them as they surface.
4. When the fruit has been softened, stir in the warmed sugar off the heat until dissolved.
5. Return to the heat, bring to the boil. Boil rapidly until setting point is reached.
6. Pour into warmed jars, cover and label.

APPLE AND GINGER JAM

Yield 4.75 kg ($10\frac{1}{2}$ lb)

2.75 kg (6 lb) cooking apples
1.15 litres (2 pints) water
grated zest and juice of 4 lemons
25 g (1 oz) root ginger, grated
or **10 ml (2 tsp) ground ginger**
3 kg (6 lb) sugar

1. Wash, peel, core and slice the apples, tying the peels and cores in a muslin bag. If root ginger is used, then it should be put in the muslin bag with the cores, etc.
2. Place the apples in the pan with the water, lemon zest and juice and the muslin bag.
3. Bring to boil, then reduce heat and simmer until fruit is tender.
4. Remove pan from the heat; take out the muslin bag and squeeze the juice from it.
5. Add the warmed sugar and stir until dissolved. Add the crystallized ginger, if used.
6. Return to the heat, bring to the boil. Boil rapidly until setting point is reached.
7. Pot in warmed jars, seal, cover and label.

Note: Fresh ginger can be peeled and frozen and used as required. It can be finely chopped in the frozen state.

AMBROSIA JAM

Yield 3.1 kg ($7\frac{1}{4}$ lb)

1 kg (2 lb) dried apricots
1 orange
2 lemons
Two 450 g (16 oz) cans crushed pineapple
sugar

1. Wash the apricots and cut into small pieces or chop coarsely in a food processor. Cover with cold water and leave to soak for 12 hours.
2. After soaking, add the finely grated rind and juice of the orange and lemons, together with the contents of the cans of pineapple.
3. Weigh the contents.
4. Place in a preserving pan, bring to simmering point, and simmer gently until the apricots are soft.
5. Remove from the heat, add 1 kg (2 lb) sugar to each 1 kg (2 lb) fruit and juice (as weighed previously); stir until dissolved.
6. Return to the heat, bring to the boil and boil rapidly until setting point is reached.
7. Pour into warmed jars, cover and label.

APRICOT JAM (FRESH FRUIT)

Yield 5 kg (10 lb)

3 kg (6 lb) fresh apricots
600 ml (1 pint) water
3 kg (6 lb) sugar

1. Wash the fruit, cut in halves and remove the stones. Crack a few stones, remove the kernels and blanch them by dipping in boiling water.
2. Place the fruit, kernels and water in a preserving pan, bring to simmering point, and simmer gently until the fruit is tender, and the contents of the pan reduced by one-third. Test for pectin.
3. Remove pan from the heat, add the sugar and stir until dissolved. Return pan to the heat, bring to the boil and boil rapidly until setting point is reached. Pour into warmed jars, cover and label.

APRICOT JAM (DRIED FRUIT)

Yield 2.5 kg (5 lb)

500 g (1 lb) dried apricots
1.75 litres (3 pints) water
juice of 1 lemon
1.5 kg (3 lb) sugar
75 g (3 oz) blanched almonds

1. Wash the apricots and cut into small pieces, or chop coarsely in a food processor. Soak in the water for 12 hours.
2. Place the fruit and water in a preserving pan, together with the lemon juice. Simmer until tender, about 30 minutes.
3. Remove from the heat, add sugar and stir until dissolved, then add almonds.
4. Return to the heat, bring to the boil. Boil rapidly until setting point is reached.
5. Pour into warmed jars, cover and label.

BANANA AND LEMON JAM

Yield 900 g ($1^{3}/_{4}$ lb)

500 g (1 lb) firm, ripe bananas, peeled
finely grated rind and juice of 3 lemons
500 g (1 lb) caster sugar

1. Peel and slice the bananas and place in a bowl. Add the grated rind and juice of the lemons, sprinkle the sugar over the fruit, cover the bowl with a plate and leave to stand until the sugar dissolves (about $1^{1}/_{2}$ hours)
2. Transfer contents of bowl to a preserving pan. Simmer gently, stirring initially to ensure sugar is dissolved, until setting point is reached (about 15-20 minutes).
3. Pour into warmed jars, cover and label.

BILBERRY JAM

Yield 1.7 kg (3 lb)

1.5 kg (3 lb) bilberries
150 ml ($^1/_4$ pint) water
1 kg (2 lb) jam sugar

1. Wash the fruit and place in a preserving pan with the water and acid. Simmer gently until the fruit is tender.
2. Add the sugar and stir until dissolved, and follow the manufacturer's instructions.
3. Pour into warmed jars, cover and label.

BLACKBERRY AND APPLE JAM

Yield 4.5 kg (10 lb)

2 lb Sugar
1 lb Blackberries
$\frac{1}{2}$ lb Apples
$\frac{1}{4}$ Pint

2 kg (4 lb) blackberries
300 ml ($^1/_2$ pint) water
3 kg (6 lb) sugar
750 g (1$^1/_2$ lb) peeled, cored and sliced cooking apples (prepared weight)

1. Pick over the blackberries and place them in a pan with half the water. Bring to the boil, then simmer until tender.
2. Place the apples in a separate pan, with the remaining water. Cook until the fruit is quite soft.
3. Mix the apple pulp and blackberries. Add the sugar and stir until it has dissolved, then bring the jam quickly to a rolling boil, and boil hard until setting point is reached.
4. Pour into warmed jars, cover and label.

SEEDLESS BLACKBERRY AND APPLE JAM

Quantities and method as above.

1. When the blackberries are tender, sieve them to remove the seeds.
2. Add the pulp to the apples, then measure and bring to the boil, stirring frequently.
3. Remove from the heat, add an equal amount of sugar, and then stir until dissolved.
4. Bring to the boil and boil hard until setting point is reached.
5. Pour into warmed jars, cover and seal.

BLACKCURRANT JAM

Yield 5 kg (10 lb)

2 kg (4 lb) blackcurrants
1.75 litres (3 pints) water
3 kg (6 lb) sugar

1. Remove the stalks and wash the fruit. Place in a preserving pan with the water. Simmer gently until the fruit is quite tender, and the contents of the pan reduced by one-third. Test for pectin. Remove from the heat.
2. Add the sugar and stir until dissolved
3. Return to the heat, bring to the boil. Boil rapidly until setting point is reached.
4. Pour into warmed jars, cover and label.

BULLACE (OR DAMSON) AND PEAR JAM

Yield 5 kg (10 lb)

1.5 kg (3 lb) prepared pears
1.5 kg (3 lb) bullaces or damsons
600 ml (1 pint) water
1 tsp citric acid
3 kg (6 lb) sugar

1. Peel and finely dice the pears. Remove stones from the bullaces or damsons.
2. Place each fruit in a separate pan with 300 ml (½ pint) water in each, and add the citric acid with the pears. Simmer gently until both fruits are tender.
3. Combine the two fruits in one pan and test for pectin. Add the sugar and stir until dissolved.
4. Return to the heat, bring to the boil. Boil rapidly until setting point is reached.
5. Pour into warmed jars, cover and label.

CHERRY JAM

Yield 1.5 kg (3 lb)

1 kg (2 lb) Morello or Mayduke cherries
800 g (1 lb 12 oz) jam sugar

1. Wash cherries and remove stones. Crack a few of the stones by wrapping in a cloth and using a weight or hammer; remove the kernels. Tie remaining stones in a muslin bag. Put cherries and juice from the lemons, plus muslin bag, into a preserving pan and heat gently.
2. When the juices begin to flow, simmer until tender. If fruit is very firm, add 3–4 tbsp of water to prevent burning. Remove muslin bag; give a good squeeze.
3. Add kernels. Add jam sugar and follow manufacturer's instructions. Skim.
4. Pot and seal.

DAMSON JAM

Yield 5 kg (10 lb)

2.4 kg ($4^{3}/_{4}$ lb) damsons
750–1.25 ml ($1^{1}/_{4}$–2 pints) water
3 kg (6 lb) sugar

1. Wash the fruit and place in a preserving pan with the water. Simmer gently until tender and the contents of the pan are reduced by one-third.
2. Remove as many stones as possible as they rise to the surface.
3. Remove from heat and test for pectin. Add sugar and stir until dissolved. Return to heat, bring to the boil. Boil rapidly until setting point is reached.
4. Pour into warmed jars, cover and label.

DAMSON AND MARROW JAM

Yield 4.5 kg (10 lb)

1.5 kg (3 lb) damsons
600 ml (1 pint) water
sugar
1.5 kg (3 lb) de-seeded and peeled marrow (prepared weight)

1. Place the damsons in a pan with half the water. Simmer gently until tender. Rub fruit through a colander to remove stones.
2. Cut the marrow into cubes of approx. 1 cm ($^{1}/_{2}$ inch) and place in a pan with the remaining water. Cook gently to a pulp.
3. Weigh and mix damson and marrow pulp. Allow 500 g (1 lb) sugar to each 500 g (1 lb) pulp. Place pulp and sugar in the pan and stir until the sugar has dissolved. Bring to rolling boil and boil hard until setting point is reached.
4. Pour into warmed jars, seal and label.

GOOSEBERRY JAM

Yield 5 kg (10 lb)

2.2 kg ($4^{1}/_{2}$ lb) gooseberries
1 litre ($1^{1}/_{2}$ pints) water
3 kg (6 lb) sugar

1. Wash, and top and tail the gooseberries. Place in a preserving pan with the water. Simmer gently until quite tender. Test for pectin. Remove from the heat.
2. Add the sugar and stir until dissolved. Return to the heat, bring to the boil and boil rapidly until setting point is reached.
3. Pour into warmed jars, cover and label.

Note: The degree of greenness of the jam will depend on the variety and maturity of the fruit, and the length of time of cooking with the sugar.

GOOSEBERRY AND ELDERFLOWER JAM

This is a variation on GOOSEBERRY JAM (above).

1. Put the flowers from 12–24 elderflower heads into a piece of scalded muslin and tie securely. Place the bundle in the pan with the gooseberries.
2. When the fruit pulp is cooked, remove the muslin and squeeze all the juice from it into the pan. Add the sugar and continue the cooking process as for GOOSEBERRY JAM.

GOOSEBERRY AND ORANGE JAM

Yield 2.5 kg (5 lb)

1.5 kg (3 lb) gooseberries
finely grated rind and juice of 2 oranges
300 ml (1/2 pint) water
1.5 kg (3 lb) sugar

1. Wash and top and tail the gooseberries and place in a preserving pan. Add the orange rind and juice, together with the water. Simmer gently until the fruit is tender. Test for pectin.
2. Remove from the heat. Add the sugar, and stir until dissolved.
3. Return to the heat, bring to the boil and boil rapidly until setting point is reached.
4. Pour into warmed jars, cover and label.

GREENGAGE JAM

Yield 4.5 kg (10 lb)

2.75 kg (6 lb) greengages
300–600 ml (1/2–1 pint) water
2.75 kg (6 lb) sugar

1. Wash, halve and stone the fruit. Place the fruit in the preserving pan with 300 ml (1/2 pint) water. Top up with extra water if necessary during cooking.
2. Use the kernels of some of the stones to add to the jam (see page 13 note 6).
3. Cook the fruit very gently, after bringing it slowly to the boil, and until tender.
4. Remove pan from heat, add sugar, stir until dissolved.
5. Return to the heat, boil rapidly until a set is achieved.
6. Pour into warmed jars, cover and label.

HIGH DUMPSIE DEARIE JAM

Yield 4.5 kg (10 lb)

1 kg (2 lb) apples
1 kg (2 lb) pears
1 kg (2 lb) plums
300 ml ($^1/_2$ pint) water
sugar
finely grated rind of 2 lemons
7–15 g ($^1/_4$–$^1/_2$ oz dried root ginger
300 ml ($^1/_2$ pint) water

1. Wash the fruit. Peel, core and finely dice the apples and pears. Remove stones from the plums. Place the fruits in a preserving pan with the water and lemon rind.
2. Bruise the ginger and tie in a muslin bag; add to the fruit.
3. Simmer gently until the fruit is tender, then remove the ginger.
4. Measure the pulp and to each litre add 600 g sugar or to each pint add 12 oz sugar. Stir until the sugar is dissolved.
5. Return the mixture to the heat, bring to the boil. Boil rapidly until setting point is reached.
6. Pour into warmed jars, cover and label.

LOGANBERRY JAM

Yield 4.5 kg (10 lb)

3 kg (6 lb) loganberries
3 kg (6 lb) sugar

1. Put the fruit in the preserving pan and heat gently until the juice starts to flow. Continue to cook over a low heat, stirring all the time until the loganberries are completely tender.
2. Remove from the heat. Add the warmed sugar and stir until dissolved.
3. Return to the heat, bring to the boil, and boil hard until the setting point is reached.
4. Pour into warmed jars, cover and label.

Note: Small quantities of this jam could be made in a Microwave.

MARROW JAM (CUBED)

Yield 4.5 kg (10 lb)

The two MARROW JAM recipes use the same quantities of ingredients but here the marrow cubes remain, while MARROW JAM (PULPED) a smooth preserve is produced. The finest marrows for preserve-making are the large greeny-gold ones that have been left to mature fully. Flavoured with root ginger and lemon, marrow can be used to make an interesting jam.

2.75 kg (6 lb) peeled and seeded marrows (prepared weight)
grated zest and juice of 4 lemons
75 g (3 oz) fresh root ginger
2.75 kg (6 lb) sugar

1. Cut marrow into cubes, approx. 1.25 cm (½ inch), and place in a steamer. Steam over boiling water until cooked and tender. Cooking time will depend on the size of the cubes but should take approx. 30 minutes.
2. Transfer the marrow to a bowl and add the lemon zest and juice.
3. Bruise ginger by placing between two sheets of greaseproof paper and hitting firmly with a weight or rolling pin.
4. Add ginger to marrow, then sprinkle all the sugar over ingredients in the bowl. Cover and leave for 24 hours.
5. Pick out the piece of ginger and tie it in a piece of scalded muslin, then place it in the pan. Add the marrow and all its juice.
6. Heat gently until the sugar is dissolved, stirring occasionally. Bring to the boil and cook until the marrow is transparent and the syrup is thick.
7. Test jam for setting point, preferably using a thermometer.
8. Remove root ginger, pot and seal.

MARROW JAM (PULPED)

Yield 4.75 kg (10½ lb)

A smooth preserve resembling a fruit butter in texture but not as thick as butter.

2.75 kg (6 lb) peeled and seeded marrow (prepared weight)
grated zest and juice of 4 lemons
225 g (8 oz) crystallized ginger, chopped
2.75 kg (6 lb) sugar

1. Cut the marrow into chunks and cook it in boiling water until tender. Drain the vegetable thoroughly, then mash it and return it to the pan.
2. Add the lemon zest and juice and the crystallized ginger. Bring the marrow to the boil, then add the sugar and stir until it has dissolved.
3. Continue to boil the jam for 20 minutes or until it is thickened. Stir occasionally to prevent it burning on the bottom of the pan.
4. Pour into warmed jars, cover and label.

MATRIMONY JAM

Yield 2.5 kg (5 lb)

500 g (1 lb) cooking apples
500 g (1 lb) pears
500 g (1 lb) Victoria plums
150 ml (1/4 pint) water
1 tsp citric acid
sugar

1. Prepare the fruit. Peel, core and dice apples and pears, and stone the plums.
2. Place the fruit in a preserving pan with the water and citric acid. Simmer gently until quite tender.
3. Measure the pulp, and to each litre of pulp add 750 g sugar or to each pint of pulp add 1 lb sugar. Stir until the sugar is dissolved.
4. Return to the heat, bring to the boil. Boil rapidly until setting point is reached.
5. Pour into warmed jars, cover and label.

MULBERRY JAM

Yield 3 kg (6 lb)

1.5 kg (3 lb) mulberries
500 g (1 lb) apples
water
1.75 kg (3 1/2 lb) sugar

1. Place the mulberries in a preserving pan, and allow to simmer in their own juices until tender.
2. Peel, core and slice the apples, place in a small amount of water in another pan and cook until soft. Mix the two fruit pulps together in the preserving pan. Add the sugar and stir until dissolved.
3. Return to the heat, bring to the boil. Boil rapidly until setting point is reached.
4. Pour into warmed jars, cover and label.

PEACH AND RASPBERRY JAM

Yield 3.5 kg (7 lb)

1 kg (2 lb) ripe peaches (weight after stoning)
1 kg (2 lb) raspberries
150 ml (1/4 pint) water
2 kg (4 lb) sugar

1. Skin, stone and chop the peaches into small pieces; crack a few stones to remove the kernels. Place peaches, raspberries and water in a preserving pan and simmer gently until tender. Remove from the heat.
2. Add the sugar, and stir until dissolved, then add a few peach kernels. Return to the heat, bring to the boil. Boil rapidly until setting point is reached.
3. Pour into warmed jars, cover and label.

PLUM JAM

Yield 5 kg (10 lb)

3 kg (6 lb) plums
300–900 ml (½–1½ pints) water
3 kg (6 lb) sugar

1. Wash the fruit and place in a preserving pan with the water. Simmer gently until the fruit is tender, and the contents of the pan reduced by one-third. Test for pectin. Remove from the heat.
2. Remove as many stones as possible as they rise to the surface.
3. Add the sugar and stir until dissolved. Return to the heat, bring to the boil and boil rapidly until setting point is reached.
4. Pour into warmed jars, cover and label.

PLUM AND ELDERBERRY JAM

Yield 3.2 kg (7 lb)

1 kg (2 lb) elderberries
300 ml (½ pint) water
1.25 kg (2½ lb) plums
2 kg (4 lb) sugar

1. Remove the stalks from the elderberries and place in a saucepan with half the water. Simmer gently until tender; strain through a jelly bag.
2. Stone the plums and cook in a preserving pan in the remaining water until tender. Add the elderberry juice. Remove from the heat.
3. Add the sugar and stir until dissolved. Return pan to the heat, bring to the boil. Boil rapidly until setting point is reached.
4. Pour into warmed jars, cover and label.

PUMPKIN/MARROW AND BLACKBERRY JAM

Yield 3 kg (5½ lb)

2 kg (4 lb) pumpkin (or marrow)
1 kg (2 lb) blackberries
600 ml (1 pint) water
2 lemons
1.7 kg (3½ lb) sugar

1. Peel the pumpkin (or marrow) and remove the seeds. Cut into small neat dice and place in a preserving pan. Wash and stalk the blackberries, add to the pumpkin, together with the water and grated rind of one lemon.
2. Simmer gently until soft, then rub through a hair or nylon sieve.
3. Return to a clean pan, add sugar, stir until dissolved. Add juice of lemons. Return pan to heat, bring to boil. Boil rapidly until setting point is reached.
4. Pour into warmed jars, cover and label.

RASPBERRY JAM

Yield 5 kg (10 lb)

3 kg (6 lb) raspberries
3 kg (6 lb) sugar

1. Place the fruit in a preserving pan and cook slowly to extract some of the juices, then simmer gently until the fruit is tender. Remove from the heat.
2. Add the sugar, and stir until dissolved. Return the pan to the heat, bring to the boil. Boil rapidly until setting point is reached.
3. Pour into warmed jars, cover and label.

RHUBARB AND GINGER JAM

Yield 2.5 kg (5 lb)

1.5 kg (3 lb) rhubarb
1.5 kg (3 lb) sugar
130 ml (4 fl oz) lemon juice
25 g (1 oz) root ginger, bruised

1. Wipe the rhubarb and cut into chunks. Place in a bowl layered up with the sugar. Add the lemon juice and leave to stand overnight.
2. Transfer to a preserving pan, and add the ginger tied in muslin.
3. Bring to the boil and boil rapidly until setting point is reached.
4. Remove the root ginger.
5. Pour into warmed jars, cover and label.

RHUBARB AND ORANGE JAM

Yield 2.5 kg (5 lb)

6 sweet oranges
sugar
1 kg (2¼ lb) rhubarb, trimmed and finely sliced

1. Scrub the oranges in warm water. Pare the zest from the oranges with a potato peeler, and cut into thin strips, or grate finely.
2. Squeeze the juice from the fruit, allowing the flesh to go with the juice. Place both the fruits and the rind in a preserving pan and cook gently until tender.
3. Weigh the pulp and to each 1 kg (2 lb) fruit add 1 kg (2 lb) sugar. Stir until the sugar is dissolved. Return the pan to the heat, and bring to the boil. Boil rapidly until the setting point is reached.
4. Pour into warmed jars, cover and label.

STRAWBERRY JAM (1)

Yield 5 kg (10 lb)

3.5 kg (7 lb) strawberries
juice of 2 lemons
3 kg (6 lb) sugar

1. Prepare the fruit, and place in a preserving pan with the lemon juice.
2. Heat gently and stir constantly until the volume is reduced by about one-third. Add the sugar and stir until dissolved.
3. Bring to the boil. Boil rapidly until setting point is reached. Remove any scum immediately; let the jam cool until a skin forms on the surface.
4. Stir gently, and pour the jam quickly into warmed jars, cover and label.

STRAWBERRY JAM (2)

Yield 2.5 kg (5 lb)

225 g (8 oz) gooseberries or redcurrants
300 ml (1/2 pint) water
1.5 kg (3 lb) strawberries
1.5 kg (3 lb) sugar

1. Place the gooseberries or redcurrants in a pan with the water and cook gently until soft. Strain off the juice.
2. Placed the prepared strawberries in a preserving pan, add the strained juice and cook gently, stirring constantly, until the fruit is soft.
3. Remove from the heat. Add the sugar and stir until dissolved.
4. Return to the heat, bring to the boil. Boil rapidly until setting point is reached.
5. Remove any scum immediately. Allow jam to cool slightly until a skin forms.
6. Pour into warmed jars, cover and label.

BLACK CHERRY CONSERVE

Yield 1.25 kg (2 1/2 lb)

1 kg (2 lb) stoned black or dark cherries
1 kg (2 lb) sugar
300 ml (1/2 pint) redcurrant juice

1. Wash and stone the cherries.
2. Dissolve the sugar in the redcurrant juice and bring to the boil.
3. Add the cherries and boil for 10 minutes, stirring constantly.
4. Drain the syrup from the cherries and return the syrup to the pan and boil hard until it begins to thicken.
5. Return the cherries to the syrup and boil again until setting point is reached. Remove any scum. Cool slightly until a skin forms.
6. Stir gently and pour into warmed jars, cover and label.

CHERRY AND ORANGE CONSERVE

Yield 2.5 kg (5 lb)

1 kg (2 lb 4 oz) black cherries
900 g (2 lb) sugar
2 large thin-skinned oranges
2 lemons
water

1. Wash and stone the cherries, crack a few stones and reserve the kernels. Wash and scrub the oranges and lemons; cut the oranges into very thin slices and remove the pips. Cut lemons in half and squeeze out the juice. Reserve it.
2. Place pips, lemon rind and cherry stones in muslin bag. Lay orange slices in large preserving pan, barely cover with water, add the bag, simmer until oranges are soft. Remove muslin bag. Add remaining ingredients. Heat gently, stirring well until the sugar has dissolved. Bring to the boil. Boil hard until a set is obtained.
3. Pour into warmed jars and seal.

PEAR AND GINGER CONSERVE

Yield 2.5 kg (5 lb)

2 kg (4 lb) hard pears
1.5 kg (3 lb) sugar
50–100 g (2–4 oz) stem ginger
2 lemons

1. Peel, core and cut the pears into quarters (eighths if large), and place in a bowl in layers with the sugar. Cover and leave to stand for 24 hours.
2. Chop ginger and add to pears with the grated rind and juice of the lemons.
3. Transfer all to a preserving pan and heat gently, stirring constantly, until all the sugar is dissolved. Bring to the boil and boil gently until the fruit is transparent and setting point is reached.
4. Cool slightly before pouring into warmed jars. Cover and label.

STRAWBERRY CONSERVE

Yield 2.7 kg (6 lb)

2 kg (4 lb) hulled strawberries
2 kg (4 lb) sugar

1. Place strawberries in layers with the sugar in a bowl and leave for 24 hours.
2. Transfer contents of the bowl to a pan, bring to the boil. Boil for 5 minutes.
3. Return to the bowl and leave for 48 hours.
4. Again transfer the mixture to a preserving pan, bring to the boil and boil for 10–20 minutes until setting point is reached.
5. Cool slightly until a skin forms. Stir gently.
6. Pour into warmed jars, cover and label.

QUINCE CONSERVE (SPICED)

Yield 1.7 kg (3½ lb)

about 450 g (1 lb) quinces
about 450 g (1 lb) oranges
1 lemon
1.25 kg (2½ lb) sugar
1 cinnamon stick
water

1. Peel, core and cut quinces into small pieces. Place in a pan with enough water to cover. Cook gently until soft. Add more water if needed to prevent burning.
2. Rub through a sieve. Place sieved pulp in a preserving pan, with the grated rinds and juice of the oranges and lemon. Add sugar and cinnamon and stir until dissolved. Bring to the boil. Boil rapidly until setting point is reached.
3. Remove cinnamon stick.
4. Pour into warmed jars, cover and label.

RASPBERRY CONSERVE

Yield 4.5 kg (10 lb)

2.5 kg (5 lb) raspberries
3 kg (6 lb) sugar

1. Place fruit in the pan and bring to the boil. Continue boiling for 10 minutes.
2. Add the warmed sugar and stir until dissolved.
3. Bring the conserve quickly to the boil and boil hard for 2 minutes.
4. Pot and seal.

Note: Quite the most delicious and truly raspberry-flavoured preserve, which does not produce a very firm set.

TOMATO AND APPLE CONSERVE

Yield 1.5 kg (2¼ lb)

500 g (1 lb) ripe tomatoes
500 g (1 lb) apples
1 lemon
750 g (1½ lb) sugar
100 g (4 oz) cut mixed peel
100 g (4 oz) stem ginger, chopped
or **50 g (2 oz) fresh ginger**

1. Skin and slice the tomatoes. Peel, core and slice the apples. Scrub the lemon, then mince it. Place all of these in a preserving pan and cook for 15 minutes.
2. Remove from the heat. Add sugar and stir until dissolved.
3. Return to the heat and simmer gently until the mixture thickens. Add peel and ginger and stir well. Continue to simmer gently for a further 10 minutes.
4. Pour into warmed jars, cover and label.

JELLIES

Jellies add variety to all meals, particularly as interesting accompaniments to many meats, or added to sauces to enrich or give a variety of flavours; for a change, when having game, why not try rowan jelly.

Jellies should be bright, clear and sparkling. They are similar to jams in the principles of making, but as only the juice is used (all traces of pulp, skin, pips being removed) considerably more fruit is required than in jam making. Damaged and windfall fruit, providing it is under-ripe, can be used (the damaged parts being cut away). Economical and interesting jellies can be made by using fruits from hedgerows.

Jellies were traditionally potted in sloping-sided jars, so that they could be turned onto a plate for serving, but as these jars are virtually unobtainable nowadays, jellies are potted in small jars, which aid setting. Jellies should be covered in the same way as jams.

It is misleading to give approximate yields for each jelly recipe, as results depend on the type and quality of the fruit used and also on the growing season.

GENERAL METHOD

1. Fruits should be washed and any unsound parts removed. It is not necessary to stalk currants or peel apples, etc., but large fruits should be cut into smaller pieces.

2. Place the prepared fruit in a large pan, adding sufficient water just to cover. The quantity of water used depends on the kind of fruit – those fruit with tough skins or hard fruits require longer cooking to soften, and therefore need more water.
3. Place the pan on the heat and simmer gently until the fruit is quite tender (about $^3/_4$–1 hour) or cook in a pressure cooker; for small quantities use a microwave.
4. Pour into a scalded jelly bag and allow to drip (about 1 hour) until there is barely any liquid dripping from it. Do *not* squeeze the jelly bag. Fruits rich in pectin can be extracted a second time – return the pulp to the pan with more water (half the original amount used) and simmer again for 30 minutes. Pour into the jelly bag and allow to drip for a further hour.
5. Test for pectin (see page 12).
6. Measure the strained juice into a preserving pan, and bring to the boil.
7. To each 600 ml (1 pint) of juice add 450 g (1 lb) sugar. Fruits rich in pectin will set 575 g ($1^1/_4$ lb) sugar to each 600 ml (1 pint).
8. Remove the pan from the heat, add sugar, and stir until dissolved.
9. Return pan to the heat, bring to the boil, and boil rapidly until setting point is reached. Recommended tests for setting point are the flake test and the temperature test (pages 13/14).
10. Remove pan from the heat, remove any scum immediately, and pour into warmed jars. Gently pouring the jelly into slightly tilted jars will help to avoid air bubbles.
11. Cover the jars immediately as for jam (page 13). Do not move the jars until the jelly has cooled.

APPLE OR CRAB APPLE JELLY

apples
ginger or cloves
water
sugar

1. Choose apples which have a definite flavour, or add flavourings such as ginger or cloves.
2. Windfall apples can be used provided the damaged portions are cut out.
3. Wash and cut up the fruit and then proceed as for GENERAL METHOD, above.
4. If spices are used, these should be whole (not ground) and cooked with the apples.

APPLE AND BLACKBERRY JELLY

1.8 kg (4 lb) blackberries
1 kg (2 lb) cooking apples
water
sugar

1. Wash the blackberries and place in a pan.
2. Wash and roughly chop the apples, removing any damaged parts. Add the apples to the blackberries. Barely cover the fruit with water. Cook gently until tender.
3. Proceed as for GENERAL METHOD (pages 29–30).

Note: The proportion of blackberries and apples can be varied according to the amount of fruit available. Wild blackberries give an excellent flavour, and apples are rich in pectin.

BLACKBERRY JELLY

4 kg (8 lb) blackberries
juice of 3 large (4 small) lemons
or **2 tsp citric or tartaric acid**
1 litre ($1^1/_2$ pints) water
sugar

1. Wash the fruit, place in a preserving pan with the lemon juice or acid and water. Simmer until tender.
2. Mash the fruit well.
3. Proceed from stage 4 of GENERAL METHOD (page 30).

BLACKCURRANT JELLY

2 kg (4 lb) blackcurrants
1.85 litres (3 pints) water
sugar

1. Wash the fruit and place in a preserving pan with 1.25 litres (2 pints) water. Simmer until tender and mash well.
2. Strain through a scalded jelly bag for 10–15 minutes.
3. Return the pulp to the pan, add another 600 ml (1 pint) water and simmer for a further 30 minutes. Then strain again.
4. Mix the two extracts together.
5. Proceed from stage 5 in the GENERAL METHOD (page 30).

DAMSON JELLY

3 kg (6 lb) damsons	**water**
	sugar

1. Wash the damsons, and place in a preserving pan. Barely cover with water. Simmer until the fruit is tender.
2. Proceed as for General Method (pages 29–30).

Note: Damsons are rich in pectin, therefore a second extraction can be made. (see page 30, note 4)

GOOSEBERRY JELLY

2 kg (4 lb) green gooseberries	**water**
(with tops and tails)	**sugar**

1. Wash the fruit and place in preserving pan. Barely cover the fruit with water. Simmer gently until the fruit is tender.
2. Proceed as for General Method (pages 29–30).

Note: A second extraction can be made (page 30, note 4). When gooseberries are ready for jelly-making, mint is at its best, and mint jelly made with gooseberries instead of apples is excellent.

GOOSEBERRY MINT JELLY

1. Follow the recipe for gooseberry jelly.
2. Proceed as for General Method (pages 29–30). After page 30, point 8, add a bunch of mint.
3. When setting point is reached, remove the bunch of mint. Add washed and chopped mint to the jelly before potting.

Note:

(a) This damp mint added will help to keep the herb suspended throughout the jelly.

(b) Green gooseberries give a brighter, clearer result.

GOOSEBERRY AND ELDERFLOWER JELLY

2 kg (4 lb) gooseberries
12 heads of elderflowers
1.25–1.75 litres (2–3 pints) water
sugar

1. Wash the gooseberries, but do not top and tail them. Place in a preserving pan with water.
2. Proceed as for GENERAL METHOD (pages 29–30).
3. Tie the elderflower heads in a muslin bag. At stage 9, plunge the heads into the boiling jelly for a few minutes. This will be sufficient to impart a muscatel flavour to the jelly.

HIP AND HAW JELLY

1 kg (2 lb) rosehips
1 kg (2 lb) hawthorn berries
juice of 4 lemons
water

Proceed as for the GENERAL METHOD (pages 29–30), adding the strained lemon juice at stage 6.

Note:
(a) If haws are ripe before the hips, they can be frozen until required.
(b) As the berries absorb a lot of water whilst softening, extra water may be required during the cooking period.

LOGANBERRY JELLY

4 kg (8 lb) loganberries
water
sugar

Prepare the fruit. Follow method as for BLACKBERRY JELLY (page 31).

MULBERRY JELLY

3 kg (6 lb) mulberries
600 ml (1 pint) water
sugar

Proceed as for GENERAL METHOD (pages 29–30).

MINT JELLY

3 kg (6 lb) green apples
juice of 4 lemons
or **2 tsp citric or tartaric acid**
water
sugar
bunch of fresh young mint
green liquid food colouring (optional)

1. Wash and cut the fruit roughly, place in a pan with lemon juice or acid and a few sprigs of the mint. Cover with water. Simmer to a soft pulp.
2. Strain through a jelly bag. Test for pectin.
3. Place the extract in a pan, bring to the boil. Add 500 g (1 lb) sugar to each 600 ml (1 pint). Stir until it is dissolved. Boil rapidly for 5 minutes.
4. Suspend the bunch of mint in the jelly and boil until setting point is reached.
5. Remove mint, add colouring (if used). Remove any scum.
6. Pour quickly into jars, cover and label.

QUINCE JELLY

2 kg (4 lb) quinces
3.5 litres (6 pints) water
sugar
15 g (1/2 oz) citric or tartaric acid (if fruit is fully ripe)

1. Wash the quinces, cut up finely and place in a large pan with 2 litres (4 pints) of the water. Cover and simmer until tender (about 1 hour).
2. Strain through a scalded jelly bag.
3. Return pulp to a pan with remaining water; make a second extract. Combine the two extracts and continue from stage 5 of GENERAL METHOD (page 30).

RASPBERRY JELLY

4 kg (8 lb) raspberries
sugar

1. Place the fruit in a large pan and heat gently until the juice runs, then mash well. Strain through a scalded jelly bag.
2. Measure the juice and add 450 g (1 lb) sugar to each 600 ml (1 pint) juice. Stir until dissolved. Return to the heat, bring to the boil and boil rapidly until setting point is reached. Remove scum.
3. Pour quickly into warmed jars, cover and label.

RASPBERRY AND APPLE JELLY

1 kg (2 lb) cooking apples (windfalls will do)
2 kg (4 lb) raspberries
water
sugar

1. Cut up the apples and place in a large pan with the raspberries and sufficient water barely to cover. Simmer until the fruit is soft. Strain through a scalded jelly bag.
2. Proceed from stage 5 of GENERAL METHOD (page 30).

REDCURRANT JELLY

3 kg (6 lb) redcurrants
1.25–1.75 litres (2–3 pints) water
sugar

1. Prepare the fruit.
2. Follow the method of making as for BLACKCURRANT JELLY (page 31).

RHUBARB AND ORANGE JELLY

1.5 kg (3 lb) rhubarb
1 kg (2 lb) oranges
2.5 litres (4 pints) water
sugar

1. Wash the fruits. Cut rhubarb into 2.5 cm (1 inch) pieces; cut oranges into 2.5 cm (1 inch) cubes. Place in a bowl with the water and leave to soak overnight.
2. Transfer the contents of the bowl to a large pan and simmer, covered, until the peel is tender (1½–2 hours). Strain through a scalded jelly bag.
3. Proceed from stage 5 of the GENERAL METHOD (page 30).

ROSEMARY JELLY

1 kg (2 lb) crab apples or windfall apples or gooseberries
water
sugar
3 sprigs fresh rosemary
1 sprig finely chopped or scissored rosemary

Follow method for MINT JELLY (page 34).

ROSEHIP AND APPLE JELLY

600 ml (1 pint) fully ripe rosehips
1.5 kg (3 lb) green apples
water
juice of 1 lemon
sugar

1. Wash the rosehips thoroughly. Place in a pan and cover with water. Simmer gently until soft, then mash with a wooden spoon.
2. Wash the apples and cut up roughly. Place in a pan and barely cover with water. Simmer gently until soft.
3. Strain the two fruits together through a scalded jelly bag.
4. Proceed from stage 5 of the GENERAL METHOD (page 30), adding the strained lemon juice with the sugar.

ROWAN JELLY

1 kg (2 lb) rowan berries
1 kg (2 lb) crab apples *or* windfall apples
water
sugar

1. Wash the berries thoroughly, removing all the leaves and twigs. Wash the apples and cut up roughly. Place both fruits in a preserving pan with sufficient water barely to cover.
2. Simmer gently to produce a pulp.
3. Strain through a scalded jelly bag.
4. Proceed from stage 5 of the GENERAL METHOD (page 30).

Note: Suitable for use with venison.

SAGE JELLY

1 kg (2 lb) crab apples
***or* windfall apples**
water
12 stems fresh sage
sugar
green liquid food colouring

1. Wash the fruit.
2. Follow the method of making as for MINT JELLY (page 34).

Note: This jelly is excellent served with pork.

MARMALADES

Marmalade is a traditional jam-like breakfast preserve made from citrus fruits, where the peel is shredded. Some other recipes use a combination of citrus fruits and other fruits, eg. apples and apricots. Some of these recipes have been included.

The principles of making marmalade are essentially the same as those for making jam, except that the peel of citrus fruits takes considerably longer to cook than the softer fruits used for jam, therefore more water is required for cooking.

1. **Pectin**
   Much of the pectin necessary for a good set is found in the pith and pips of citrus fruits, and although in all finished marmalade no pips are wanted, and in some the absence of pith and pips makes a far more appetising result, it is essential that the pith and pips are cooked to extract pectin.

2. **Acid**
   As citrus fruits contain a much higher proportion of pectin than other fruits, extra acid must be added to obtain a good set. Add acid as follows: to 1.5 kg (3 lb) fruit add the juice of 2 lemons or 1 tsp citric or tartaric acid.

GENERAL METHOD

1. Scrub the fruit. Prepare according to the recipe. Simmer fruit with the water and acid until the peel is tender (about 2 hours). Remove from the heat.
2. Remove the bag containing the pips. Carry out the pectin test (page 12).

3. Add the sugar and stir until dissolved. Return to the heat, bring to the boil and boil until the setting point is reached (see tests for setting point on page 13).
4. Remove from the heat and carefully skim off any scum. Allow to cool for 15–20 minutes until a skin forms. This cooling helps prevent the shreds from rising in the jar when potted. Gently stir in the skin. Pour into warmed jars and cover as for jams (see page 13). Label with type and date. Store in a cool, dry, dark, well-ventilated place.

   Note: Prepared, canned oranges can be purchased. These are an excellent standby. Follow the recipe on the can.

Seville oranges

Seville oranges are available in January and February for a very short season, and it is advisable to make batches of marmalade at this time. Seville oranges can be scrubbed and frozen in containers in suitable amounts for making into marmalade at a later date. Alternatively, oranges can be cooked and frozen with the juice, ready for later addition of sugar. Always make sure that you carefully label containers, giving the contents and details of the amount of sugar required.

Marmalades with alcohol

If a marmalade containing alcohol is your choice, when potting the finished marmalade add a tablespoon of your chosen liquor to each 450 g (1 lb) jam jar, and stir with great care to distribute the flavour. In this way a variety of flavours can be added to a single batch of marmalade.

When a yield of 5 kg (10 lb) of Seville orange marmalade is to be produced, add as follows for these varieties:

Ginger marmalade

225 g (8 oz) chopped, preserved ginger added after the sugar has dissolved.

Whisky marmalade

Add 4 fl oz (10 tbsp) whisky to the marmalade just before potting.

Brandy marmalade

Add 4 fl oz (10 tbsp) brandy to the marmalade just before potting.

APRICOT MARMALADE

Yield 4.5 kg (9 lb)

500 g (1 lb) dried apricots
750 g (1½ lb) Seville or sweet oranges
grated rind and juice of 1 lemon
1.8 litres (3 pints) water
3 kg (6 lb) sugar
25 g (1 oz) split almonds (optional)

1. Wash the apricots. Place in a bowl and cover with 1.2 litres (2 pints) water. Leave to soak for 24 hours.
2. Transfer contents of the bowl to a preserving pan, add the grated rind and juice of the lemon and simmer gently until tender, stirring occasionally.
3. Scrub and pare the oranges. Shred finely. Halve oranges and squeeze out the juice. Tie roughly chopped pith and pips in a muslin bag. Cook in pressure cooker with 600 ml (1 pint) water. Bring slowly to 15 lb pressure (HIGH) and cook for 20 minutes. Allow to cool 10 minutes before opening.
4. Alternatively, cook in an open pan with at least 1.2 litres (2 pints) water for about 2 hours or until the peel is soft.
5. Squeeze the muslin bag to extract the juice, then remove the bag from the pan. Combine the two fruit pulps. Carry out a pectin test (page 12).
6. Add sugar. Stir until dissolved. Return to heat, bring to boil. Boil until the setting point is reached. Stir in the almonds.
7. Pour into warmed jars, cover and label.

CARROT MARMALADE

Yield 4.5 kg (9 lb)

500 g (1 lb) peeled carrots
500 g (1 lb) oranges
500 g (1 lb) lemons
3.5 litres (6 pints) water
3 kg (6 lb) sugar
1 tsp ground cinnamon

1. Finely chop the carrots and place in a preserving pan. Scrub the fruit. Peel and shred the zest finely. Cut the fruit in half and squeeze out the juice. Chop the pith roughly and place with the pips in a muslin bag. Place the finely shredded peel, juice and muslin bag in the pan with the carrots. Add the water and simmer gently for 1½–2 hours, until the peel is soft.
2. Squeeze the muslin bag to extract the juice and remove the bag. Remove from the heat and test for pectin (page 12).
3. Add sugar and stir until dissolved. Stir in cinnamon. Return pan to the heat, bring to boil. Boil rapidly until setting point is reached. Remove the scum.
4. Allow to cool until a skin begins to form. Stir gently.
5. Pour into warmed jars, cover and label.

DARK THICK MARMALADE

Yield 5 kg (10 lb)

1 kg (2 lb) Seville or bitter oranges
2 lemons
2.75–3.5 litres (4½–6 pints) water
3 kg (6 lb) sugar
25 g (1 oz) black treacle

1. Follow the method as for SEVILLE ORANGE MARMALADE (1) (page 45) but the lemons should be sliced and included in the pulp.
2. Add the treacle with the sugar.

GRAPEFRUIT MARMALADE

Yield 5 kg (10 lb)

Either **1 kg (2¼ lb) grapefruit**
and 350 g (12 oz) lemons
Or **1.5 kg (3 lb) grapefruit**
and 2 tsp citric or tartaric acid
2.75–3.5 litres (4½–6 pints) water
3 kg (6 lb) sugar

1. Scrub fruit, pare zest and shred finely. Cover with water and cook in a small saucepan until the shreds are tender, approx. 1 hour.
2. Coarsely chop the rest of the fruit and the pith and place with the remaining water in a pan. Cover and simmer gently for about 1½ hours.
3. Strain through a colander, or rub through a sieve to make a thick marmalade. Add the strained pulp to the peel. Carry out a pectin test.
4. Add the sugar and stir until dissolved.
5. Return to the heat, bring to the boil and boil rapidly until setting point is reached. Remove any scum.
6. Allow to cool until a skin forms. Stir gently.
7. Pour into warmed jars, cover and label.

ALTERNATIVE METHOD

1. as before.
2. Place whole fruit, muslin, acid and water in an oven-proof casserole and cook in the slow oven of a solid fuel fuel cooker for 4 hours or until tender.
3. Strain liquid into a preserving pan. Cut fruit in quarters. Remove pips and pith into a small pan. Cover with some of the cooking liquid. Boil for 5 mins to extract the pectin. Strain liquid back into the preserving pan.
4. Chop the fruit and add with the zest to the preserving pan. Test for pectin.

Continue as point 4 above.

JELLY MARMALADE

Yield 2.25 kg (5 lb)

1 kg (2 lb) Seville oranges
2.75 litres (4½ pints) water
juice of 2 lemons
1.5 kg (3 lb) sugar

1. Scrub fruit, pare zest and shred the zest finely. Cook the shreds in a small saucepan with 300 ml (½ pint) of the water, approx. 1 hour.
2. Coarsely chop the rest of the fruit and place in another pan with the lemon juice and the remaining water. Simmer gently for 2 hours.
3. Drain the liquid from the shreds on to the pulp and strain through a scalded jelly bag. Do not squeeze.
4. A second extraction can be made as for jelly, see page 30). Carry out a pectin test.
5. Place the strained juice in a pan with the sugar and stir until dissolved. Add the shreds. Return the pan to the heat, bring to the boil and boil rapidly until setting point is reached. Remove any scum.
6. Allow to cool until a thick skin forms. Stir gently.
7. Pour into warmed jars, cover and label.

LEMON & GINGER MARMALADE (THICK)

Yield 5 kg (10 lb)

1.5 kg (3 lb) lemons
100–175 g (4–6 oz) preserved ginger, chopped
3 litres (5–6 pints) water
3 kg (6 lb) sugar

1. Scrub the fruit, place in a covered pan with the water and simmer gently for about one hour, until the lemons are soft.
2. Retaining the liquid in the pan, remove the lemons and cut the fruit in half. Remove the pips, tie these in a muslin bag and return to the pan. Slice the fruit and return it to the pan.
3. Return the uncovered pan to the heat and then simmer gently for about 30 minutes, or until the original volume has been reduced by about one-third.
4. Remove the pan from the heat and carry out a pectin test (page 12).
5. Add the sugar and stir until dissolved. Chop the ginger finely and add to the pan. Return pan to the heat, bring to the boil. Boil rapidly until setting point is reached.
6. Remove any scum. Cool slightly until a skin is formed. Stir gently.
7. Pour into warmed jars, cover and label.

LEMON OR LIME MARMALADE *Yield 5 kg (10 lb)*

1.5 kg (3 lb) lemons or limes
2.75–3.5 litres (4½–6 pints) water
3 kg (6 lb) sugar

Follow the method of making as for GRAPEFRUIT MARMALADE (page 40).

LEMON AND GRAPEFRUIT MARMALADE *Yield 3 kg (6 lb)*

1 kg (2¼ lb) lemons
3.5 litres (6 pints) water
1 large grapefruit
granulated sugar

1. Wash and pare the lemons. Remove pith. Cut the zest into hair strips and put into a small pan with 600 ml (1 pint) of the water. Cover and simmer until soft.
2. Chop lemon, grapefruit and pith. Put into a preserving pan with remaining 3 litres (5 pints) water. Cover and simmer until fruit is soft, approx. 2 hours.
3. Drain liquid from strips into preserving pan.
4. Strain contents of preserving pan through a jelly bag. Measure the liquid. For every 600 ml (1 pint) allow 450 g (1 lb) warmed sugar.
5. Return the liquid to the pan and bring to the boil and add the warmed sugar and the strips of lemon peel, stirring until the sugar has dissolved. Bring to the boil and boil rapidly until set, about 15 minutes.
6. Leave to cool a little and stir well before potting, to distribute the peel.
7. Pour into warmed jars, cover and label.

LEMON AND WHISKY MARMALADE *Yield 2.5 kg (5 lb)*

750 g (1½ lb) lemons
1.5 litres (2½ pints) water
1.5 kg (3 lb) sugar
1 miniature bottle whisky
or **3 fl oz (5 tbsp)**

1. Scrub lemons, cut in half and squeeze out juice. Place pips in a muslin bag. Slice fruit finely, place in a preserving pan with juice, muslin bag and water. Simmer gently until tender, approx. 2 hours. Squeeze muslin bag to extract juice, then remove the bag. Test for pectin. Remove from the heat.
2. Add the sugar and stir until dissolved. Return to the heat. Bring to the boil and boil rapidly until setting point is reached. Stir in the whisky.
3. Remove any scum. Allow to cool slightly until a skin is formed. Stir gently.
4. Pour into warmed jars, cover and label.

LIME MARMALADE

Yield 5 kg (10 lb)

1.5 kg (3 lb) lemons or limes
2.75–3.5 litres ($4^{1/2}$–6 pints) water
3 kg (6 lb) sugar

Follow the method of making as for GRAPEFRUIT MARMALADE (see page 40).

LIME AND LEMON MARMALADE

Yield 2.5 kg (5 lb)

0.75 kg ($1^{1/2}$ lb) fruit (limes and 1 lemon)
1.35 kg (3 lb) sugar
1 litre (2 pints) water

PRESSURE COOKER METHOD

1. Prepare fruit and place in pressure cooker with water. Bring pan to HIGH (15 lb) pressure. Lower heat and maintain this pressure for 10-15 minutes. Leave pressure to reduce slowly at room temperature before opening cooker.
2. When cool, place the cooked fruit in a colander over a small container to collect any spare liquid. Cut each of the fruits into 4 pieces, scrape out the flesh and chop. Remove any pips and the long white shreds from the pith. Peel and chop peel finely. Place in pressure cooker pan and put pips and white shreds in small sauce pan. When all the fruit has been prepared, boil up the pips, etc., and strain liquid into the pan. Bring liquid to boiling point.
3. Remove from the heat. Stir in the warmed sugar. Return to the heat.
4. Proceed as for GENERAL METHOD no.3 (page 38).

Note:

(a) This recipe can be followed if a jam pan is used – the water quantity needs to be doubled and the cooking time at least 2 hours at simmering point.

(b) The addition of one lemon, for total weight of fruit 0.75 kg ($1^{1/2}$ lb), gives a better set than using all limes. Too many lemons destroy the flavour.

THREE FRUIT MARMALADE

Yield 5 kg (10 lb)

1.5 kg (3 lb) fruit, consisting of:
2 grapefruit
4 lemons
2 sweet oranges
2.75–3.5 litres ($4^{1/2}$–6 pints) water
3 kg (6 lb) sugar

Follow the method of making as for GRAPEFRUIT MARMALADE (page 40).

PINEAPPLE MARMALADE

Yield 3 kg (6 lb)

1 lemon
3 large Jaffa oranges
525 g (1 lb 3 oz) can pineapple
1.5 litres ($2^1/_2$ pints) water
2 kg (4 lb) sugar

1. Scrub lemon and oranges and peel as for eating. Cut peel into small cubes. Coarsely chop the fruit, tying pips in a muslin bag. Place all in a preserving pan, cover with water and strained pineapple juice. Simmer gently until peel is tender.
2. Squeeze the muslin bag to extract the juice, then remove the bag. Carry out a pectin test (page 12). Remove the pan from the heat.
3. Add sugar and stir until dissolved; add pineapple cut into small cubes. Return pan to the heat, bring to boil. Boil rapidly until setting point is reached.
4. Remove any scum. Allow to cool until a skin is formed. Stir gently.
5. Pour into warmed jars, cover and label.

RAPID CHEAT ORANGE & APRICOT MARMALADE

Yield 3.5 kg (7 lb)

100 g (4 oz) dried apricot pieces
750 ml ($1^1/_4$) pints) boiling water
2.25 kg (5 lb) granulated sugar
850 g (1 lb 14 oz) can prepared Seville oranges

1. Cut the apricot pieces into smaller pieces. Pour over boiling water, cover and leave to soak in a warm place for one hour.
2. Pour contents of the can of oranges and sugar into a large preserving pan, add apricots and soaking water. Heat preserving pan gently, stirring until the sugar has dissolved. Turn up the heat and boil rapidly for approx 10 minutes.
3. Test for set. Cool for about 10 minutes.
4. Pour into warmed jars, cover and label.

SATSUMA & GRAPEFRUIT MARMALADE

Yield 2.5 kg (5 lb)

1 kg ($2^1/_4$ lb) fruit, consisting of:
1 grapefruit ***and*** **1 lemon**
satsumas
$1^1/_2$ litres (3 pints) water
1.5 kg (3 lb) sugar

1. Scrub fruit and place in pressure cooker.
2. Follow method for LIME MARMALADE (2), (page 43)

SEVILLE ORANGE MARMALADE (1)

Yield 5 kg (10 lb)

1.5 kg (3 lb) Seville oranges
2.75–3.5 litres ($4^{1/2}$–6 pints) water
3 kg (6 lb) sugar
juice of 2 lemons or 1 tsp citric or tartaric acid

EITHER follow the method of making as for GRAPEFRUIT MARMALADE (page 40) but it is not necessary to remove any pith from the peel unless very thick.

OR ...

1. Scrub the fruit, cut in half and squeeze out the juice. Tie the pips in a muslin bag. Slice the peel thinly, without removing the pith. Place in a preserving pan with the juice, the muslin bag and the water. Simmer gently until the peel is quite soft and the contents are reduced by about one-third, approx. 2 hours.
2. Remove from the heat, squeeze the muslin bag to extract the juice, then remove the bag. Test for pectin. Add the sugar and stir until dissolved.
3. Return the pan to the heat, bring to the boil, and boil rapidly until setting point is reached.
4. Remove any scum. Allow to cool slightly until a thin skin forms. Stir gently.
5. Pour into warmed jars, cover and label.

SEVILLE ORANGE MARMALADE (2)

Yield 2.5 kg (5 lb)

750 g ($1^{1/2}$ lb) Seville oranges
juice of 1 lemon
1 litre ($1^{1/2}$ pints) water
1.5 kg (3 lb) sugar

1. Prepare the fruit as for SEVILLE ORANGE MARMALADE (1) above.
2. Place the prepared fruit and lemon juice in the pressure cooker pan with the water. Put on the lid, leaving the vent open. Heat gently and when steam appears, close the vent and bring to 15 lb (HIGH) pressure. Maintain the pressure for 20 minutes, then allow the pan to cool at room temperature for 10 minutes.
3. Remove the bag of pips after extracting the juice. Test for pectin (page 12).
4. Add the sugar and stir until dissolved. Return the open pan to the heat, bring to the boil and boil rapidly until setting point is reached.
5. Remove any scum. Allow to cool until a skin is formed. Stir gently.
6. Pour into warmed jars, cover and label.

SEVILLE ORANGE MARMALADE (3)

Yield 2.5 kg (5 lb)

625 g ($1^{1/2}$ lb) Seville oranges
juice of 1 lemon
1.25 litres (2 pints) water
1.5 kg (3 lb) sugar

1. Use whole fruit and cook in a pressure cooker (see page 43, recipe 2).
2. Place cooked fruit in a colander, over a small saucepan, to collect spare liquid.
3. Cut each of the oranges into 4 pieces, remove the pips and place in the small saucepan. Chop up the fruit pulp and finely chop the peel. Return to the pressure cooker.When all the fruit has been prepared, bring the pips to boiling point and simmer for a few minutes to extract the pectin.
4. Strain liquid from pips into cooker. Bring pulp to boiling point, remove from heat. Add warmed sugar, stir to dissolve, bring to boiling point while continuing to stir, boil rapidly. Test for set. Cool slightly.
5. Pour into warmed jars, cover and label.

TANGERINE JELLY MARMALADE

Yield 2.25 kg (5 lb)

1.25 kg ($2^{3/4}$ lb) fruit, consisting of:
1 grapefruit *and* **1 lemon** *and* **tangerines**
2.5 litres ($4^{1/2}$ pints) water
1.4 kg (3 lb) sugar

1. Prepare all the fruit, pare the zest from the tangerines and shred finely. Put in a muslin bag. Chop the rest of the fruit and place in the preserving pan with the water. Add the muslin bag. Bring to the boil and simmer for 30 minutes.
2. Remove muslin bag and cook the rest of the fruit for a further $1^{1/2}$ hours.
3. Strain the pulp through a jelly bag. Pour into a clean pan. Bring to the boil.
4. Add the sugar and stir until it dissolves. Add tangerine zest and bring to a rolling boil. Boil rapidly. Test for set. Skim, stand and stir the marmalade.
5. Pour into warmed jars, cover and label.

TANGERINE & LIME MARMALADE

Yield 2.5 kg (5 lb)

1 kg ($2^{1/4}$ lb) tangerines
4 limes
1.75 litres (3 pints) water
900 g (2 lb) granulated sugar

1. Scrub fruit, squeeze out all the juice. Remove pips and tie in a muslin bag. Shred peel and remaining pulp very finely. Put peel, fruit, bag and juice into preserving pan with the water and bring to boil. Simmer until peel is soft, 1–$1^{1/2}$ hours.
2. Remove from heat. Add warmed sugar, stirring well until dissolved. Bring to boil. Boil rapidly until set is obtained, approx. 5 mins. Cool slightly Stir gently.
3. Pour into warmed jars, cover and label.

BUTTERS AND CHEESES

Butters and cheeses are an ideal way of using up an excess of fruit. Fruit cheeses are served in exactly the same way as dairy cheeses – cut into wedges and served with, or instead of, dairy cheese with biscuits or bread and butter. Fruit butters and cheeses are made when there is a glut of fruit. Although they contain a large quantity of sugar, the proportion is less than that in jams.

Fruit butters

These are of a softer consistency than cheeses and are usually spiced and should be hermetically sealed. They are usually served as a spread.

Cheeses

These are cooked to a stiff consistency and set in small moulds so that they can be turned out for serving and cut into wedges.

GENERAL METHOD

1. Wash the fruit, cut up if necessary, and place in a saucepan with sufficient water barely to cover. Simmer gently until soft. Sieve.

2. **To make a cheese:**
   To each 500 g (1 lb) pulp add 500 (1 lb) sugar. Stir until sugar is dissolved. Boil gently for 3/4–1 hour, stirring occasionally to prevent burning until a clean line is left when a spoon is drawn across. Pour into a mould which has been smeared with glycerine so that the cheese will turn out.

3. **To make a butter:**
   To each 500 g (1 lb) pulp add 250–375 g (8–12 oz) sugar. Stir until the sugar is dissolved, add any spices and cook gently until a thick creamy consistency is reached. Pour into jars with airtight covers. Then process by immersing in a deep pan of hot water. Bring to the boil and boil for 5 minutes.

APPLE BUTTER

3 kg (6 lb) crab apples or windfalls
1.25 litres (2 pints) water
1.25 litres (2 pints) cider
sugar
1 tsp ground cinnamon
1 tsp ground cloves

1. Wash the apples and chop roughly, removing any damaged parts. Place in a pan with the water and cider. Cook gently until soft.
2. Sieve. Return the sieved pulp to the pan and simmer to obtain a thick consistency.
3. To each 500 g (1 lb) pulp add 350 g (12 oz) sugar. Stir until the sugar is dissolved. Boil, stirring frequently until a thick, creamy consistency is obtained.
4. Pour into warmed jars, seal and process as for GENERAL METHOD (page 47).

APRICOT BUTTER WITH SPICES

1 kg ($2^{1}/_{4}$ lb) fresh ripe apricots
90 ml (6 tbsp) water
grated zest and juice of 2 lemons
225 g (8 oz) caster sugar for every 600 ml (1 pint) purée
5 ml (1 tsp) blend of ground cinnamon, cloves and allspice per 600 ml (1 pint) purée

1. Wash, halve and stone the fruit. Put the fruit into a pan and simmer until tender.
2. Pass through a coarse sieve or liquidise.
3. Measure the purée and add appropriate amounts of sugar and spices.
4. Grate the zest from the lemons and put with the juice, purée, sugar and the spices into the pan. Cook slowly, stirring continuously until the mixture is very thick.
5. Pot, seal and process as for GENERAL METHOD (page 47).

AMERICAN PLUM GUMBO

1.5 kg (3 lb) plums
300–600 ml (½–1 pint) water
2 small oranges
1.5 kg (3 lb) sugar
500 g (1 lb) seedless raisins

1. Wash the plums and, if very large, halve or quarter them. Place in a pan with the water and simmer until a pulp is formed.
2. Scrub the oranges and slice thinly, removing the pips.
3. Sieve the plums and place the sieved purée in a pan with all the other ingredients.
4. Cook over a low heat to dissolve the sugar. Continue cooking, stirring occasionally, until a thick pulp is obtained.
5. Pour into warmed jars, cover and label.

BRAMBLE CHEESE

1.5 kg (3 lb) blackberries
1.5 kg (3 lb) cooking apples
water
sugar

1. Wash the blackberries. Wipe the apples and chop up roughly. Place both in a pan with sufficient water barely to cover. Cover and cook gently until reduced to a pulp.
2. Rub through a sieve. Return the sieved pulp to an open pan and cook further, if necessary, to reduce the pulp until thick.
3. Weigh the pulp. To each 500 g (1 lb) pulp add 500 g (1 lb) sugar and cook over a low heat to dissolve the sugar. Continue cooking until a thick consistency is obtained. When a spoon is drawn across the base of the pan, it should leave a clean line.
4. Pour into prepared moulds. Cover as for jam (page 13).

QUINCE CHEESE

quinces
sugar
water

1. Prepare quinces by washing and cutting into small pieces.
2. Follow the method as for Bramble Cheese (above).

CRANBERRY CHEESE

1 kg (2 lb) cranberries
600 ml (1 pint) water
500 g (1 lb) sugar per 500 g (1 lb) pulp

1. Wash the cranberries and put them in a preserving pan with the water. Simmer until they pop and are soft.
2. Pass through a fine sieve. Return to the pan and heat gently. Add the warmed sugar and continue to cook gently, stirring well, until the paste is very thick and leaving the sides of the pan.
3. Pot and seal.

DAMSON CHEESE

3 kg (6 lb) damsons
300 ml (½ pint) water
sugar

Follow the method for Bramble Cheese (page 49).

PLUM AND APPLE CHEESE

1.5 kg (3 lb) cooking apples
500 g (1 lb) plums
water
sugar

1. Wash and cut up the apples without peeling. Wash the plums, and halve or quarter if large. Place both the fruits in a closed pan with sufficient water barely to cover.
2. Proceed as for Bramble cheese (page 49).

VINEGAR PRESERVES

Here is a varied choice of pickles, some of the old favourites and also some interesting new ones. Flavoured vinegars are also included – fruit vinegars to help fight that tickling cough in winter and herb vinegars to give additional flavour to salad dressings.

Vinegar preserves allow for great individual scope. These preserves are mixtures of fruits and vegetables flavoured with spices, with sugar and vinegar acting as the preservatives. The vinegar used must be a good quality one containing not less than 5% acetic acid. Owing to the nature of vinegar, great care must be taken in the choice of containers and covers. The cover must be one that will prevent vinegar from evaporating and yet also be unaffected by the acidity in the vinegar. The most suitable tops today are twist tops which have a plastic lining. Wax circles and cellophane tops are *not* suitable.

As vinegar preserves have such a variety of ingredients mixed together, it is necessary to keep them for a few weeks before using, to ensure a good blend of flavours. It is recommended that pickles should be kept for 6 weeks before using, and chutneys for 2–3 months. There are a few, however, which can be used almost immediately but they will also improve further if allowed to mature.

The spices that can be used are many, and the personal choice of these adds greatly to the individuality of the finished preserve. Both whole and ground spices can be used but if a clear, bright result is required, you must use whole spices tied in a muslin bag which can be removed before the preserve is potted.

Whatever spices are used, remember that they should be fresh each year, as their strength diminishes during storage.

Vinegars

Flavoured vinegars are often required in cookery, and it is very easy, and usually cheaper, to make these at home. Top quality vinegar, containing 5% acetic acid, is required. Brown malt vinegar is usually used but some light-coloured pickles require the use of white, or distilled, malt vinegar. Cider or wine vinegars can be used but their flavour is often masked by strong flavours in some pickles and they are expensive.

Spiced vinegars

These can be purchased but it is more fun to spice your own. Recommended quantities: to each 1 litre (2 pints) malt vinegar add 25 g (1 oz) mixed whole spices (cloves, cinnamon sticks, blade mace, allspice in equal amounts). If a hotter flavoured vinegar is required a few peppercorns and 2–4 chillies may be added.

Cold Spiced Vinegar

This gives the best results but needs plenty of forethought. Place the whole spices in the cold vinegar in the bottle and allow to steep for 4–8 weeks. Occasional shaking helps the full flavour to be extracted.

Hot Spiced Vinegar

Place vinegar and whole spices in a bowl covered with a plate, over a saucepan of cold water. Bring the water slowly to the boil, then remove the pan from the heat. Allow the spices to steep in the vinegar for 2 hours. Strain and bottle.

Sweetened spiced vinegar

1.75 litres (3 pints) malt vinegar
450 g (1 lb) brown sugar
7.5 ml ($1\frac{1}{2}$ tsp) salt
5 ml (1 tsp) pickling spice
5 ml (1 tsp) black peppercorns
2.5 ml ($\frac{1}{2}$ tsp cloves

Put all ingredients in a saucepan, stir over low heat until sugar is dissolved. Simmer for 5 mins. Pour into a china bowl. Allow to steep for 2 hours as above.

Herb vinegars

Half-fill a wide-necked jar with freshly gathered leaves, picked just before flowering. Fill to the top with white vinegar and alow to steep for at least 14 days in a warm place before use. Strain vinegar. Bottle and place a few sprigs of herb/flower in bottle. Store in a cool dark place.

Fruit vinegars

Use equal quantities of fruit – usually soft fruit (eg. blackberries, raspberries) and a good malt vinegar, ie. 500 g (1 lb) fruit to 600 ml (1 pint) vinegar. Place in a bowl, cover and leave to steep for 3–5 days, stirring occasionally. Strain off liquid, measure, and to each 600 ml (1 pint) add 500 g (1 lb) white sugar. Stir over a gentle heat until sugar is dissolved. Bring to boil. Boil for 10 minutes. Put into bottles and seal.

Pickles

There are two types: clear pickles, eg. onions, and sweet pickles, eg. damsons.

Clear pickles

It is necessary when making clear pickles to salt or brine the vegetables for 12–18 hours to extract some of the water from them. Sea salt is preferable to vacuum-packed salt as it is less dense but it is advisable to weigh salt to ensure that the vegetables are not oversalted. For a cold brine use 500 g (1 lb) salt to 4.5 litres (1 gallon) water. The method is as follows:

(a) Prepare vegetables, cut into bite-sized pieces and place in a bowl. Cover with brine, or alternatively sprinkle layers with salt. Cover vegetables with a plate to ensure they are under the liquid. Leave 12–48 hours in a cool place.
(b) Rinse the vegetables carefully. Drain thoroughly.
(c) Pack into jars and cover with spiced vinegar, ensuring that there is at least 1 cm (1/2 inch) vinegar over the vegetables.
(d) Cover the jars tightly with a vinegar-proof top page 13).

Sweet pickles

These are made from fruit and/or sweet vegetables. The fruit is stewed gently in sweetened, spiced vinegar until tender. Whole fruits need to be pricked before cooking to avoid shrivelling during storage.

PICKLED APRICOTS

1 kg (2 lb) fresh apricots
1 kg (2 lb) sugar
600 ml (1 pint) white spiced vinegar (see page 52)

1. Dissolve sugar in the vinegar. Prepare fruit by cutting in half, removing the stones, and cooking in a little water until just beginning to soften. Drain well.
2. Place in a sweetened spiced vinegar. Simmer gently for about 3/4 hour, until just tender – do *not* to overcook. Drain from syrup and pack neatly into jars.
3. Place the syrup back on the heat and boil to reduce to a thick syrup.
4. Pour over the fruit in the jars, cover and label.

PICKLED BEETROOT

1 kg (2¼ lb) raw beetroot
1.15 litres (2 pints) malt vinegar
4 tbsp honey
juice of 1 large lemon

1. Wash and cook the beetroot in boiling salted water. Allow to cool. Peel, slice or dice or leave whole if small.
2. Place the vinegar, honey and lemon juice in a preserving pan. Bring to boiling point and boil for one minute. Cover and leave to cool.
3. Pack the beetroot into jars and cover with the strained vinegar. Seal carefully.

PICKLED RED CABBAGE

red cabbages
salt
spiced vinegar (page 52)

1. Choose cabbages which are firm and a good red colour. Remove the core and slice finely. Place in a bowl, sprinkling salt between each layer. Leave to stand for 24 hours. Drain under cold running water and rinse well. Drain again, ensuring all surplus water is removed.
2. Pack loosely into jars. Cover with cold spiced vinegar. Cover securely and label.

Note: This pickle is ready for eating in one week, and at its best if eaten before three months, after which it will lose its crispness.

PICKLED CUCUMBER

Yield 2.3 kg (5 lb)

3 kg (6 lb) sliced cucumber, unpeeled
250 g (8 oz) salt
2.5 litres (4 pints) water
1.8 litres (3 pints) white vinegar
1 tbsp celery seed
2 tbsp mustard seed
1½ tsp curry powder
1 kg (2 lb) sugar

1. Place prepared cucumber in a bowl. Mix salt and water, pour over cucumber and leave for at least 6 hours – preferably overnight. Rinse and drain thoroughly.
2. Place the remaining ingredients in a pan, heat gently until the sugar is dissolved, stirring frequently. Bring to the boil.
3. Add the cucumber slices, return to the boil, and simmer gently for 4–5 minutes, stirring constantly.
4. Pack into warmed jars, cover securely and label.

PICKLED DAMSONS (1), PEACHES OR PEARS

3.5 kg (8 lb) damsons, hard pears or firm peaches
1 litre (2 pints) vinegar
2 kg (4 lb) sugar
$^1/_2$ lemon, peeled zest
15 g ($^1/_2$ oz) whole cloves
15 g ($^1/_2$ oz) whole allspice
7 g ($^1/_4$ oz) fresh root ginger
7 g ($^1/_4$ oz) cinnamon stick

1. Wash the damsons and remove the stalks. Prick thoroughly. Peel, core and quarter the pears or cut in eighths if they are large. Peel and halve or quarter the peaches, discarding the stones.
2. Tie the lemon peel and spices in a muslin bag. Place them in a preserving pan. Add the vinegar and sugar and heat until the sugar has dissolved, stirring continuously. Add the prepared fruit and simmer until tender but not too soft.
3. Remove the bag of spices and drain the fruit.
4. Pack fruit into warmed jars.
5. Pour syrup back into the pan and bring to the boil. Boil the syrup until it is reduced and slightly thick. Pour over the fruit. Cover.
6. Reserve any leftover syrup for topping up the liquid in the jars (use twist top jars), as the fruit tends to absorb the liquid on standing. The fruits are best if allowed to mature for at least a month.

Note: These pickled fruits are excellent with cold meats.

PICKLED DAMSONS (2)

Ingredients as above for PICKLED DAMSONS (1)

1. Wash the damsons, remove the stalks, prick and then place them in a bowl.
2. Pour on hot, sweetened, spiced vinegar and leave the fruit to soak for 5–7 days, keeping it submerged by putting a plate on top.
3. Drain the fruit. Re-boil the vinegar and pour it over the damsons again.
4. Leave the fruit for 5–7 days, then repeat the boiling.
5. After a further week, pack the damsons into jars and boil the vinegar until slightly thickened.
6. Pour the hot vinegar over the fruit and cover the jars.

Note: A longer method but the damsons tend to retain their shape better.

MILITARY PICKLE

Yield 4 kg (8 lb)

1 marrow
1 cucumber
1 cauliflower
500 g (1 lb) runner beans
500 g (1 lb) onions
salt
7 chillies
15 g (½ oz) turmeric
15 g (½ oz) ground ginger
75–100 g (3–4 oz) plain flour
2.5 litres (4 pints) vinegar
500 g (1 lb) demerara sugar

1. Prepare the vegetables, and cut into bite-sized pieces. Place them in a bowl, sprinkle with salt and leave overnight. Rinse in cold water and drain very thoroughly.
2. Blend the spices and flour together with a little vinegar to form a smooth paste.
3. Place the vegetables, vinegar and sugar in a pan, heat gently until the sugar is dissolved, then bring to the boil and boil for 5 minutes.
4. Add the blended spices, return to the boil, stirring constantly. Boil for 30 minutes.
5. Pack into warmed jars, cover securely and label.

PICCALILLI (SHARP & HOT)

Yield 3 kg (6 lb)

3 kg (6 lb) prepared vegetables –
diced cucumber, marrow, beans, small onions, cauliflower florets green tomatoes (if liked)
500 g (1 lb) cooking salt
4.5 litres (1 gal) water (optional)
15 g (½ oz) turmeric
25–40 g (1–1½ oz) dry mustard
25–40 g (1–1½ oz) ground ginger
150 g (6 oz) white sugar
1.2 litres (2 pints) white vinegar
20 g (¾ oz) cornflour or plain flour

1. Prepare the vegetables and brine or salt them as described under *Clear Pickles* on page 53.
2. Rinse thoroughly under cold running water and drain.
3. Mix together the spices and the sugar in a large pan, and stir in most of the vinegar.
4. Add the prepared vegetables and simmer gently until the desired texture is obtained – either crisp or tender. Do *not* cook until soft.
5. Blend the cornflour or flour with the rest of the vinegar and add to the other ingredients.
6. Bring back to the boil and, stirring carefully, boil for 2–3 minutes.
7. Pack into warmed jars, cover securely and label.

MIXED PICKLE

A selection of:

small onions or shallots
cauliflower, cucumber
marrow, runner beans
brine
spiced vinegar (page 52)

1. Prepare vegetables and cut into bite-sized pieces. Place in a bowl and cover with brine (page 53). Stand for 24–48 hours. Wash and drain thoroughly.
2. Pack neatly into jars and cover with cold spiced vinegar.
3. Cover securely and label.

MUSTARD PICKLE WITH GREEN BEANS

1 kg (2 lb) green beans
750 g (1½ lb) onions
1 litre (1½ pints) malt vinegar
pinch of salt
25 ml (1½ tsp) turmeric
5 ml (1 tsp) dry mustard
750 g (1½ lb) demerara sugar
45 g (1½ oz) cornflour

1. Cook beans in salted water. Strain and mince.
2. Mince the onions. Cook until tender in 300 ml (½ pint) of the vinegar.
3. Add the beans and the remaining vinegar. Boil for 15 minutes.
4. Blend cornflour, turmeric and dry mustard with a little vinegar to form thick paste. Add to bean and onion mixture, with sugar. Boil for another 10 minutes.
5. Cool, pot, seal and label.

PICKLED NASTURTIUM SEEDS

Use as a substitute for capers.

3 peppercorns
1 bay leaf
½ tsp salt
300 ml (½ pint) white vinegar
unripe nasturtium seeds

1. Place the spices and vinegar in a pan and simmer gently for 30 minutes. This vinegar may be prepared in advance and stored in a securely covered bottle.
2. Pick unripe nasturtium seeds on a fine day, wash and dry thoroughly. Place on greaseproof paper on a tray and leave in the sun for 3–5 days to dry thoroughly, or place in cool oven. Put in small jars and cover with prepared vinegar.
3. Cover the jars securely, label and leave for 2 months.

PICKLED ONIONS

small onions
salt
water
spiced vinegar (page 52)

1. Choose small, even-sized onions. Place in a bowl. Make a brine using 500 g (1 lb) salt to 4.5 litres (1 gal.) water. Pour over onions and leave for 12 hours. Drain.
2. Peel onions and place in some freshly made brine. Leave for 24 hours. They will float – put a plate on top to keep them submerged. Drain and rinse thoroughly, removing surplus moisture. Pack into bottles. Cover with cold spiced vinegar.
3. Cover and label.

SPICED CRAB APPLES

Yield 1.5 kg (3 lb)

1.5 kg (3 lb) crab apples
600 ml (1 pint) vinegar
1 kg (2 lb) sugar
5 cm (2 inch) cinnamon stick
6 cloves
1 heaped tsp pickling spice

1. Place the vinegar and sugar in a pan with the spices (tied in a muslin bag). Heat gently to dissolve the sugar, stirring occasionally, and then allow to simmer gently for 10 minutes.
2. Prepare the fruit by washing and de-stalking. Prick thoroughly and, if large, cut in half. Place in the sweetened vinegar and simmer gently until tender.
3. Strain off the vinegar, and pack the fruit into bottles.
4. Return vinegar to the pan and reduce to half by rapid boiling. Pour over fruit.
5. Cover the jars, label and store.

SWEET PICKLED PRUNES

Yield 1.5 kg (3 lb)

500 g (1 lb) dried prunes
1.25 litres (2 pints) sweetened spiced vinegar

1. Soak the prunes in water overnight.
2. Prepare the sweetened spiced vinegar as for PICKLED DAMSONS (page 55).
3. Place drained prunes in a pan with vinegar and simmer until tender (take care not to break the prunes). Remove prunes from vinegar and pack into jars.
4. Boil the vinegar until reduced to a syrup consistency, and pour into the jars to cover the prunes.
5. Cover securely, label and store for at least 4 weeks before eating.

SPICED ORANGES OR LEMONS

Yield 700 g ($1^3/_4$ lb)

6 oranges or lemons
water
575 g ($1^1/_4$ lb) white sugar)
450 ml ($^3/_4$ pint) white vinegar
1 tsp whole cloves
5 cm (2 in) stick of cinnamon
1 tsp blade mace

1. Scrub the oranges or lemons and slice thickly. Place in a pan with sufficient water to cover. Bring to the boil and simmer gently until tender, approx. $1^1/_2$–2 hours. Drain.
2. Dissolve the sugar in the vinegar over a gentle heat and add the spices. Simmer for 10 minutes.
3. Add the drained fruit, and simmer gently for about 1 hour.
4. Strain off the vinegar. Pack the oranges into warmed jars. Then return the vinegar to the pan and boil rapidly to reduce to a syrup. Pour over the oranges.
5. Cover securely, label and store.

SPICED QUINCES

1 kg (2 lb 4 oz) large ripe quinces
50 g (2 oz) sea salt
white sugar
wine vinegar
coriander seeds

1. Wash, peel, core and cut quinces into eighths. Put the fruit into a saucepan and cover with cold water. Bring to boiling point and boil for 10 minutes. Drain in a colander.
2. Put the peel and cores into another pan. Cover with cold water. Cook until tender. Strain through a jelly bag. Measure the juice, and to each 600 ml (1 pint) add 450 g (1 lb) sugar plus 150 ml ($^1/_4$ pint) vinegar and 5 ml (1 tsp) coriander. Return these ingredients to a stainless steel pan with the juice and bring gently to the boil. Add the quinces and simmer until tender.
3. Pour the fruit juice, etc., into a china bowl, cover and leave to stand overnight.
4. The next day, drain off the syrup, return it to the pan and bring to the boil. Pour over the fruit, cover and leave overnight.
5. The next day, drain off the syrup and return to the pan, bring to the boil and boil until it is reduced and thick.
6. Pack the fruit into jars, cover with the hot syrup, and seal.

PICKLED WALNUTS

Walnuts should be pickled when they are green and not fully formed. They are usually at this stage of development in June or early July. The walnuts must be used before they have any shells, which begin to form opposite the stalk, about 5 mm (1/4 inch) away from the end. Prick them with a needle or stainless steel fork. If there is evidence of a shell forming, they should be discarded.

Green walnuts
Sweetened spiced vinegar (page 52)
brine *(see page 53)*
5 ml (1 tsp) black peppercorns
2.5 ml (1/2 tsp) whole cloves

1. Place the walnuts in a bowl and pour in enough brine to cover. Put a plate on top to keep the walnuts submerged. Soak them for several days. Change the brine and soak the nuts for another week.
2. Drain the nuts and spread them out on trays lined with kitchen paper. Leave the nuts in a warm atmosphere until they turn black; this will be about one day.
3. Pack the blackened walnuts into jars. Cover them with the sweetened spiced vinegar (page 52) and put on the lids.
4. Leave to mature for at least a month before using.

Notes:

(a) Unsweetened, spiced vinegar (page 52) can be used instead of the sweetened vinegar.

(b) Always wear rubber gloves when dealing with walnuts. The stain is difficult to remove.

CHUTNEYS

Chutneys add greatly to the choice of accompaniments to serve with cold meats and cheese. Spicy tomato chutney is superb with cheese, and a homemade mango chutney is excellent with curry.

A chutney is a vinegar preserve which offers great scope for individuality by the maker. It is a mixture of fruits, fresh and dried, vegetables, sugar, vinegar and spices, cooked slowly together to form a thick jam-like consistency. Making chutney could be described as carrying out a rescue operation, because windfall fruits and mis-shapen vegetables can be used provided the damaged parts are removed. In a finished chutney, although some vegetables may retain a slightly crisp texture, there should be no 'free' vinegar floating at the top of the jar. A good chutney should have a mellow, mature flavour.

Care should be taken towards the end of cooking time, to avoid the chutney burning on the base of the pan; occasional stirring and a low temperature help. Chutneys should be poured into jars, filled to within 5 mm ($^{1}/_{4}$ inch) of the top and covered as for other vinegar preserves (page 51).

Vinegar has a slight hardening effect on some ingredients, especially onions and apples, so it is advisable to cook these ingredients in a little water to soften them before adding the rest of the ingredients.

Chutneys should be stored for 2–3 months before eating, although some of the present-day recipes, which tend to be rather mild, will be ready for eating almost at once. However, they lack character compared with the well-matured chutneys.

APPLE CHUTNEY

Yield 2.5 kg (5 lb)

1.5 kg (3 lb) sour apples
1 kg (2 lb) onions
500 g (1 lb) seedless raisins
750 g ($1^{1}/_{2}$ lb) brown sugar
finely grated rind and juice of 2 lemons
50 g (2 oz) fresh ginger
1 tbsp mustard seed
1 tsp salt
$^{1}/_{4}$ tsp pepper
1.25 litres (2 pints) vinegar

1. Peel and core the apples. Peel the onions.
2. Mince the apples, onions and raisins, and place in a preserving pan.
3. Add grated lemon rind and strained juices and rest of ingredients. Bring to boil. Simmer gently, stirring occasionally, until desired consistency is reached.
4. Pour into warmed jars, cover and label.

APPLE AND APRICOT CHUTNEY

Yield 3.1 kg (7 lb)

250 g (8 oz) dried apricots
2 kg (4 lb) cooking apples
500 g (1 lb) onions
500 g (1 lb) sultanas
500 g (1 lb) soft brown sugar
750 ml (1 pint) vinegar
1 tbsp salt
$^{1}/_{4}$ tsp cayenne pepper

1. Place apricots in a bowl with cold water to cover and leave to soak overnight.
2. Peel, core and chop the apples. Peel and chop onions. Drain and chop apricots and sultanas. Place all ingredients in a preserving pan, bring to boil. Stir until the sugar is dissolved. Simmer gently until desired consistency is reached.
3. Pour into warmed jars, cover and label.

GINGER CHUTNEY

Yield 2 kg (4 lb)

300 g (10 oz) root ginger, peeled and finely chopped
350 g (12 oz) red pepper, chopped
225 g (8 oz) courgette, chopped
225 g (8 oz) raisins or sultanas
350 g (12 oz) onions, chopped
4 lemons, chopped, pips removed
1 litre ($1^{3}/_{4}$ pints) vinegar
450 g (1 lb) dark brown sugar
10 ml (2 tsp) salt

1. Put all ingredients except sugar into a preserving pan. Bring mixture to boil. Reduce heat and simmer until ingredients are tender, approx. 30–40 minutes.
2. Add sugar, stir until dissolved. Simmer 35–45 minutes, until chutney is thick.
3. Pot, cover and label.

BANANA CHUTNEY

Yield 1.8 kg (4 lb)

450 g (1 lb) onions
125 g (4 oz) crystallized ginger
225 g (8 oz) stoned or block dates
8 ripe bananas (medium sized)
15 g (½ oz) mixed pickling spice
2 tsp salt
300 ml (½ pint) vinegar
225 g (8 oz) black treacle

1. Peel the onions and mince together with the ginger and dates. Place in a preserving pan. Mash the bananas and add to the pan. Tie pickling spices in a muslin bag and add to the pan together with the rest of the ingredients.
2. Bring to boil, stir until black treacle is dissolved, simmer gently until desired consistency is reached. Remove bag of spices.
3. Pour into warmed jars, cover and label.

CUCUMBER AND APPLE CHUTNEY

Yield 2.7 kg (5 lb)

1 kg (2 lb) cooking apples
675 g (1½ lb) onions
900 g (2 lb) cucumber
600 ml (1 pint) vinegar
450 g (1 lb) demerara sugar
15 g (½ oz) salt
½ tsp cayenne pepper

1. Peel, core and chop the apples. Peel and finely chop the onion. De-seed the cucumber; if ridge variety, peel as well. Chop finely. Place apple, onion and cucumber in a pan with vinegar, bring to boil and simmer gently until soft.
2. Add sugar, salt and cayenne. Heat gently, stirring until sugar is dissolved, then continue simmering until the desired consistency is reached.
3. Pour into warmed jars, cover and label.

GOOSEBERRY CHUTNEY

Yield 2 kg (4½ lb)

1. **1.5 kg (3 lb) gooseberries, topped and tailed**

250 g (8 oz) onions, peeled
300 ml (½ pint) water
500 g (1 lb) sugar
15 g (½ oz) salt
1 tbsp ground ginger
or **50 g (2 oz) root ginger, peeled and grated**
½ tsp cayenne pepper
600 ml (1 pint) vinegar

1. Mince or finely chop gooseberries and onions. Place in a covered pan with the water and cook until soft. Add rest of ingredients, bring to boil, stirring until sugar is dissolved, and continue cooking until desired consistency is reached.
2. Pour into warmed jars, cover and label.

DAMSON CHUTNEY

Yield 2.7 kg (6 lb)

2 kg (4 lb) damsons
750 g (1½ lb) apples
4 onions
750 g (1½ lb) raisins
3 cloves garlic
2 tbsp salt
2 litres (3 pints) vinegar
1 kg (2 lb) demerara sugar
25 g (1 oz) root ginger
25 g (1 oz) whole allspice
2 tsp whole cloves

1. Wash the damsons, place in a covered pan with a little water, and cook until soft. Remove the stones.
2. Meanwhile, peel apples and onions, either chop finely or mince. Mince the raisins. Crush garlic with the salt. Bruise ginger and tie in a muslin bag with the other spices. Place all ingredients in a preserving pan, bring to boil, stirring until sugar is dissolved, simmer gently until desired consistency is reached.
3. Pour into warmed jars, cover and label.

GREEN TOMATO CHUTNEY

Yield 3 kg (7¼ lb)

2 kg (4 lb) green tomatoes
500 g (1 lb) apples
250 g (8 oz) stoned raisins
625 g (1¼ lb) shallots
15 g (½ oz) root ginger
8–10 chillies
2 tsp salt
500 g (1 lb) brown sugar
600 ml (1 pint) vinegar

1. Chop the tomatoes, peel and chop the apples and shallots, and chop the raisins – *or*, mince all the fruit. Bruise the ginger and tie in a muslin bag with chillies.
2. Place all the ingredients in a preserving pan, bring to the boil, stirring until the sugar is dissolved, and simmer until the desired consistency is reached. Remove the muslin bag.
3. Pour into warmed jars, cover and label.

MARROW AND APPLE CHUTNEY

Yield 3.5 kg (7 lb)

2 kg (4 lb) marrow
75 g (3 oz) salt
1 kg (2 lb) sour apples
500 g (1 lb) shallots
30 g (1 oz) bruised ginger, chillies and peppercorns, mixed
500 g (1 lb) sugar
2 litres (3 pints) vinegar

1. Peel and cut the marrow into small pieces; layer up in a bowl with the salt between the layers. Leave for 12 hours, then drain.
2. Peel, core and chop the apples. Peel and chop the shallots. Tie the spices in a muslin bag. With the exception of the sugar and vinegar, place all the ingredients in a preserving pan. Bring to boil and simmer gently until tender.
3. Add the sugar and vinegar, stir until the sugar is dissolved and simmer until the desired consistency is reached. Remove the muslin bag.
4. Pour into warmed jars, cover and label.

MARROW CHUTNEY

Yield 1.5 kg (3 lb)

500 g (1 lb) marrow (prepared weight)
1 tbsp salt
500 g (1 lb) onions
500 g (1 lb) tomatoes
125 g (4 oz) sultanas
250 g (8 oz) sugar
3 chillies
3 cloves
1 pinch mixed spice
300 ml (1/2 pint) vinegar

1. Prepare the marrow and cut into small cubes, place in a bowl, sprinkle with the salt and leave for 24 hours. Drain.
2. Peel and chop onions and tomatoes. Place all ingredients in a preserving pan, including marrow, and bring to the boil. Stir until sugar is dissolved and simmer gently until tender and desired consistency is reached.
3. Pour into warmed jars, cover and label.

MIXED FRUIT CHUTNEY

Yield 3.5 kg (7 lb)

2 kg (4 lb) apples
500 g (1 lb) gooseberries
and 500 g (1 lb) green tomatoes
or **1 kg (2 lb) green tomatoes**
500 g (1 lb) onions
1.5 litres (2 pints) vinegar
25 g (1 oz) pickling spice
250 g (8 oz) sultanas
750 g (1 1/2 lb) brown sugar
25 g (1 oz) salt

1. Peel, core and chop the apples. Prepare the gooseberries and chop. Slice the tomatoes, and peel and chop the onions. Place these ingredients in a preserving pan with half the vinegar and simmer gently until soft.
2. Tie the pickling spice in a muslin bag and add with the remaining ingredients to the fruit pulp and bring back to the boil.
3. Stir until the sugar is dissolved and then simmer gently until the desired consistency is reached. Remove the muslin bag.
4. Pour into warmed jars, cover and label.

MANGO CHUTNEY

Yield 2 kg (4 lb)

1 kg (2 lb) fresh mangoes
750 g (1½ lb) cooking apples
125 g (4 oz) onions
250 g (8 oz) stoned dates
125 g (4 oz) raisins
juice of 1 large lemon
600 ml (1 pint) vinegar
25 g (1 oz) salt
7 g (¼ oz) cayenne pepper
¼ tsp nutmeg
3 bay leaves
1½ tbsp lime juice
125 g (4 oz) tamarinds (optional)
1 kg (2 lb) demerara/Barbados sugar

1. Peel and quarter the mangoes. Peel, core and chop the apples. Peel and chop the onions. Roughly chop the dates and raisins. Place all the ingredients except the lime juice and sugar in a large bowl, mix thoroughly and leave to stand for at least 3 hours.
2. Transfer to a preserving pan, bring to boil. Simmer gently until tender, stirring frequently. Add sugar and lime juice, stir until sugar is dissolved, and continue to simmer until thick and of desired consistency.
3. Pour into warmed jars, cover and label.

PEAR, DATE AND NUT CHUTNEY

Yield 1.5 kg (3½ lb)

1.5 kg (3 lb) pears
125 g (4 oz) seedless raisins
125 g (4 oz) stoned dates
250 g (8 oz) walnut halves
350 ml (1¼ pint) wine vinegar
250 g (8 oz) brown sugar
juice of 3 lemons
2 tsp salt

1. Peel, core and chop the pears. Chop the raisins, dates and walnuts.
2. Place all the ingredients in a preserving pan, bring to the boil, stirring until the sugar is dissolved, and then simmer gently until tender and the desired consistency is reached.
3. Pour into warmed jars, cover and label.

PLUM CHUTNEY

Yield 3 kg (6 lb)

1.5 kg (3 lb) plums
500 g (1 lb) onions
500 g (1 lb) apples
500 g (1 lb) sultanas
250 g (8 oz) sugar
25 g (1 oz) salt
1 tsp ground cinnamon
1 tsp ground allspice
1 tsp ground ginger
pinch cayenne pepper
1 litre (1½ pints) vinegar

1. Stone the plums and chop roughly. Peel and chop the onions. Peel, core and chop the apples and chop the sultanas. Place all ingredients in a preserving pan, bring to the boil, stirring until the sugar is dissolved and then simmer gently until tender and the mixture has reached the desired consistency.
2. Pour into warmed jars, cover and label.

PUMPKIN CHUTNEY

Yield 1.8 kg (4 lb)

1.1 kg (1½ lb) pumpkin
600 ml (1 pint) vinegar
900 g (2 lb) sugar
225 g (8 oz) seedless raisins
125 g (4 oz) onion, chopped
25 g (1 oz) salt
1 tsp ground ginger
1 tsp pepper
¼ tsp ground nutmeg
juice of 1 lemon
1½ tbsp grape juice
4 bay leaves

1. Prepare the pumpkin and chop into small dice. Place in a bowl with 300 ml (½ pint) vinegar and the other ingredients, mix well, cover and leave for 3 hours.
2. Transfer to a preserving pan, bring to boil, stirring until sugar is dissolved. Simmer gently for about one hour. Add remaining vinegar and continue cooking until desired consistency is reached.
3. Pour into warmed jars, cover and label.

RHUBARB CHUTNEY

Yield 2.2 kg (4 lb)

1 kg (2 lb) rhubarb
2 lemons
25 g (1 oz) garlic
25 g (1 oz) root ginger
500 g (1 lb) sultanas
1 kg (2 lb) brown sugar
1 tsp curry powder
½ tsp cayenne pepper
600 ml (1 pint) vinegar

1. Slice the rhubarb finely and place in a preserving pan. Squeeze the juice from the lemons and strain onto the rhubarb. Crush the garlic and add to the pan. Bruise the ginger and tie in a muslin bag together with the lemon skin.
2. Place the remainder of the ingredients in the pan, bring to the boil, stirring until the sugar is dissolved. Simmer gently until the desired consistency is reached. Remove the muslin bag.
3. Pour into warmed jars, cover and label.

RIPE TOMATO & APPLE CHUTNEY

Yield 2.5 kg (5 lb)

1 kg (2 lb) apples (prepared weight)
1 kg (2 lb) ripe tomatoes, skinned
½ kg (1 lb) brown sugar
250 g (½ lb) chopped onion
125 g (¼ lb) mustard seed
25 g (1 oz) salt
250 g (½ lb) raisins
25 g (1 oz) ground ginger
25 g (1 oz) garlic
½ tsp cayenne pepper
1 litre (1½ pints) malt vinegar

1. Cook onions, tomatoes and apples in 300 ml (½ pint) of vinegar for 30 mins.
2. Add rest of ingredients and cook for a further hour, stirring at regular intervals.
3. Pour into warm jars. Seal. Matures on storage. Better if stored at least 6 months.

SPICY TOMATO CHUTNEY

Yield 1.8 kg (4 lb)

500 g (1 lb) ripe tomatoes
500 g (1 lb) onions, peeled
500 g (1 lb) cooking apples
2 cloves garlic
1 large green pepper
300 ml (½ pint) vinegar
375 g (12 oz) brown sugar
1 tbsp salt
1 tbsp paprika
2 tsp prepared mustard
1 tsp chilli powder
1 tsp Worcestershire sauce
175 g (6 oz) tomato purée
¼–1 tsp cayenne pepper (to taste)

1. Dip the tomatoes in boiling water for half to one minute. Remove skins and chop the flesh. Place in a saucepan.
2. Chop or coarsely grate the onions; peel, core and slice the apples; crush garlic and de-seed and chop green pepper. Add onions, apples, garlic and peppers to tomatoes with half the vinegar. Cover and simmer until onions are soft.
3. Add the remaining ingredients, bring to the boil and stir until the sugar is dissolved. Simmer uncovered until the desired consistency is reached.
4. Pour into warmed jars, cover and label.

ORANGE CHUTNEY

Yield 2.5 kg (5 lb)

500 g (1 lb) onions
1 kg (2 lb) cooking apples
2 kg (4 lb) sweet oranges
500 g (1 lb) sultanas or seedless raisins
1 tbsp salt
2 tsp ground ginger
2 tsp cayenne pepper
2.5 litres (4 pints) vinegar

1. Peel and chop the onions, place in a covered pan with a little water and cook gently until tender.
2. Peel, core and chop the apples. Add to the pan. Continue cooking gently.
3. Scrub the oranges and peel, removing as much white pith as possible. Mince the peel and pulp. Place all the ingredients, except the sugar, with half the vinegar in a preserving pan and simmer gently until the orange peel is tender.
4. Add the sugar and remaining vinegar, bring to the boil, stirring until the sugar is dissolved; continue simmering until the desired consistency is reached.
5. Pour into warmed jars, cover and label.

THREE FRUIT CHUTNEY

Yield 2.3 kg (5 lb)

250 g (8 oz) dried apricots
1 kg (2 lb) marrow, prepared weight
20 g (3/4 oz) salt
1 kg (2 lb) apples, prepared weight
15 g (1/2 oz) mustard seed
75 g (3 oz) preserved ginger, chopped
750 g (1 1/2 lb) demerara sugar
1 tsp turmeric
2 tsp cornflour
1/2 tsp garlic, finely chopped
1/2 tsp cayenne pepper
1 litre (1 1/2 pints) vinegar

1. Place the apricots in a bowl, cover with water and soak for 24 hours.
2. Prepare the marrow, cut into small cubes, place in a bowl, sprinkle with the salt and leave to stand overnight. Drain well.
3. Drain the apricots and chop finely. Peel, core and chop the apples and place in a preserving pan with the apricots, marrow and a little water. Cover and simmer until a pulp is obtained.
4. Tie the mustard seed in a muslin bag.
5. Add all the remaining ingredients and the muslin bag to the pan, bring to the boil, stirring until the sugar is dissolved, then continue to simmer, uncovered, until the desired consistency is reached. Remove the muslin bag.
6. Pour into warmed jars, cover and label.

OLD DOWER HOUSE CHUTNEY

Yield 7 kg (14 lb)

1.5 kg (3 lb) plums, stoned
2 kg (4 lb) apples, weighed after peeling
500 g (1 lb) tomatoes, red or green
1 kg (2 lb) seedless raisins
500 g (1 lb) onions
1.5 kg (3 lb) demerara sugar
15 g (1/2 oz) garlic
7 g (1/4 oz) chillies
125 g (4 oz) salt
3 tbsp ground mixed spice
750 ml (1 pint) vinegar
125 g (4 oz) crystallized ginger *or* **60 g (2 oz) fresh ginger (finely chopped)**

1. Cut up the plums and tomatoes and put into the pan with half the vinegar and cook slowly, stirring all the time.
2. Mince the remainder of the fruit and vegetables and add to the pan. Add the sugar, salt and spices and cook very slowly, stirring carefully. Simmer for at least one hour.
3. Add the rest of the vinegar and cook gently for 10 minutes.
4. Pot and seal.

RED AND GREEN PEPPER CHUTNEY

Yield 3 kg (6 lb)

500 g (1 lb) red and green peppers, mixed
1 kg (2 lb) sour apples
750 g (1 1/2 lb) onions
1 kg (2 lb) green tomatoes
25 g (1 oz) salt
1 litre (1 1/2 pints) vinegar
500 g (1 lb) sugar
40 g (1 1/2 oz) bruised ginger, chillies, whole cloves, whole allspice, mustard seed, and peppercorns, mixed.

1. Cut the peppers in half, and remove the stalks and seeds.
2. Peel and core the apples; peel the onions.
3. Mince or finely chop the peppers, tomatoes, apples and onions.
4. Place in a preserving pan.
5. Tie the spices in a muslin bag. Add to the pan with half the vinegar. Bring to the boil and simmer gently until thick.
6. Add the remaining vinegar and the sugar, bring back to the boil, stirring until the sugar is dissolved, and continue simmering until the desired consistency is reached.
7. Pour into warmed jars, cover and label.

SAUCES AND RELISHES

As an accompaniment to any meal or as an extra ingredient in casseroles, home-made sauces are ideal. Relishes have arrived from the United States – they offer interesting textures and flavours, and many may be eaten immediately.

Sauces

Sauces are made from similar ingredients to those in chutneys, but they are sieved part-way through cooking, to obtain a purée. If a good, bright colour is required, as in a ripe tomato sauce, the sugar is not added until a short time before the end of cooking.

Sauces made from ingredients with a low acid content, such as ripe tomatoes, require to be sterilised after potting, to avoid fermentation. Fill the bottles to within 2.5 cm (1 inch) of the top and screw the tops lightly into place. Place the bottles in a large, deep pan, with hot water reaching up to their necks, bring to the boil and allow to simmer for 30 minutes. After removing from the water, tighten up the tops, cool and label.

Relishes

Relishes are a mixture of fruit and/or vegetables with spices and vinegars. The method of preparation of relishes is such that the vegetables retain some of their crispness, through little or no cooking. Because the quantity of vinegar used is low, relishes *cannot* be considered as true preserves. They can be eaten immediately and most should not be kept longer than 6–8 weeks. They are a delightful accompaniment to salads and cold meats.

BEETROOT RELISH

Yield 1.8 kg (4 lb)

1 kg (2 $^{1}/_{4}$ lb) raw beetroot
50 g (2 oz) fresh ginger
zest and juice of 4 lemons
800 g (1 $^{3}/_{4}$ lb) granulated sugar
10 g (4 oz) blanched and slivered almonds

1. Wash and peel the uncooked beetroot and put it through a coarse mincer. Place it in a heavy pan and barely cover with water. Boil and then simmer for about one hour, until just tender. Drain.
2. Chop the ginger. Add lemon zest and juice, ginger and sugar to the beetroot. Stir well, heating gently until the sugar has dissolved. Boil 3 mins.
3. Remove from the heat. Stir in the almonds and seal.

BEETROOT AND HORSERADISH

Yield 1.5 kg (3 lb)

500 g (1 lb) beetroot
250 g (8 oz) horseradish relish
pinch of salt
125 g (4 oz) sugar
300 ml ($^{1}/_{2}$ pint) white wine vinegar

1. Boil the beetroot until tender, peel and shred.
2. Wash horseradish; grate across sticks to avoid getting long shreds. Mix together beetroot, horseradish, salt and sugar. Add wine vinegar. Mix thoroughly.
3. Place in jars, cover and label. Ready for immediate use. Will keep about 4 weeks.

BLACKBERRY KETCHUP

blackberries
water

To each 600 ml (1 pint) pulp add:
$^{1}/_{2}$ tsp salt
125 g (4 oz) sugar
$^{1}/_{4}$ tsp dry mustard
$^{1}/_{8}$ tsp ground cinnamon
$^{1}/_{8}$ tsp ground cloves
$^{1}/_{8}$ tsp ground nutmeg
300 ml ($^{1}/_{2}$ pint) vinegar

1. Place blackberries in a pan with sufficient water to reach halfway up the fruit. Simmer until quite soft. Sieve through a nylon sieve, and measure the pulp.
2. Place the measured pulp in a saucepan with all the other ingredients. Simmer for about 30 minutes or until the desired pouring consistency is reached.
3. Pour into warmed bottles, cover and label.

CHILLI SAUCE

Yield 6 x 300 g (12 oz) jars

450 g (1 lb) onions, peeled and chopped
450 g (1 lb) apples, peeled and chopped
450 g (1 lb) tomatoes, skinned and chopped
225 g (1/2 lb) sultanas, chopped
2 cloves garlic, peeled and crushed
or **15 ml (1 tbsp) garlic paste**
225 g (1/2 lb) sugar
600 ml (1 pint) cider or wine vinegar

Bruise the following and tie in a muslin bag:
10 ml (2 tsp) sea salt
10 ml (2 tsp) whole mustard seed
10 ml (2 tsp) whole allspice
10 whole or 6 fresh chillies, sliced

1. Cook all ingredients together in a preserving pan until mixture is creamy. Take care to prevent sticking and burning. Remove the muslin bag.
2. Liquidise or sieve the mixture. Return to the pan, bring to the boil.
3. Pot and seal.

Note: A really hot sauce, suitable for barbecues. The sauce can be made hotter or milder by increasing or reducing the chillies.

CORN AND PEPPER RELISH

Yield 1.75 kg (3 1/2 lb)

750 g (1 1/2 lb) sweetcorn kernels
2 large onions
2 red peppers
2 green peppers
2 tsp salt
2 tsp plain flour
1 tsp turmeric
2 tsp dry mustard
250 g (8 oz) white sugar
600 ml (1 pint) white vinegar

1. Place the sweetcorn in a pan containing 1 cm (1/2 inch) lightly salted, boiling water. Bring to the boil and boil for 3 minutes. Drain well.
2. Peel and chop the onions. De-seed and chop the peppers. Mix the salt, flour, turmeric, mustard and sugar together in a pan and blend in the vinegar.
3. Add the sweetcorn, peppers and onions and stir well. Bring to the boil, and simmer gently for 30 minutes, stirring occasionally.
4. Pour into jars, cover and label.

CUCUMBER & GREEN PEPPER RELISH *Yield 1.1 kg ($2^1/_4$ lb)*

750 g ($1^1/_2$ lb) ridge cucumbers
250 g (8 oz) onion
1 green pepper
18 g ($^3/_4$ oz) salt
300 ml ($^1/_2$ pint) white vinegar
150 g (5 oz) sugar
1 tsp turmeric
1 tsp mustard seed
1 tsp ground allspice
$^1/_2$ tsp ground mace

1. Peel and dice the cucumbers, finely slice the onions and de-seed and shred the pepper. Place in a bowl with the salt. Leave to stand for 3 hours.
2. Drain, rinse in cold water and drain again thoroughly.
3. Place remaining ingredients in a pan, stir until sugar is dissolved, bring to boil and simmer for 2 minutes. Add the drained vegetables, bring to the boil, and simmer for 4–5 minutes, stirring constantly.
4. Pour into jars, cover securely and label.

GOOSEBERRY SAUCE *Yield 1.3 litres (2 pints)*

1.5 kg (3 lb) gooseberries
350 g (12 oz) onions
1 tsp ground ginger
1tsp cayenne pepper
$^1/_2$ tsp salt
600 ml (1 pint) vinegar
500 g (1 lb) sugar

1. Wash the gooseberries. Peel and slice the onions. Place together in a pan with the spices, salt and half the vinegar, bring to the boil and cook until soft.
2. Sieve pulp and return to a clean pan. Stir in sugar and the rest of the vinegar. Cook gently until a creamy consistency is obtained, stirring occasionally.
3. Pour into bottles, seal and label.

MUSHROOM KETCHUP *Yield 1.1 litres (2 pints)*

1.8 kg (4 lb) mushrooms
100 g (4 oz) salt
$1^1/_2$ tsp allspice
$1^1/_2$ tsp black peppercorns
$1^1/_2$ tsp ginger
1 tsp cloves
1 tsp mustard seed
600 ml (1 pint) vinegar

1. Break mushrooms into pieces, sprinkle with salt and leave to stand overnight.
2. Rinse carefully. Mash with a wooden spoon.
3. Place all ingredients in a pan, cover, bring to boil and cook for about 30 minutes.
4. Strain into bottles and seal. Sterilise, as described on page 71.

PLUM SAUCE

Yield 2 litres (3½ pints)

4 kg (8 lb) plums
500 g (1 lb) onions
250 g (8 oz) currants
15 g (½ oz) root ginger, bruised
15 g (½ oz) whole allspice
7 g (¼ oz) chillies
7 g (¼ oz) peppercorns
7 g (¼ oz) mustard seed
1.2 litres (2 pints) vinegar
500 g (1 lb) sugar
50 g (2 oz) salt

1. Cut up the plums, peel and chop the onions. Place together in a pan with the currants, spices and 600 ml (1 pint) vinegar. Bring to the boil and simmer for 30 minutes.
2. Rub the pulp through a sieve and return to a clean pan. Add the sugar, salt and remaining vinegar, bring back to the boil, and simmer for one hour or until a creamy consistency is obtained.
3. Pour into warmed bottles, seal and label.

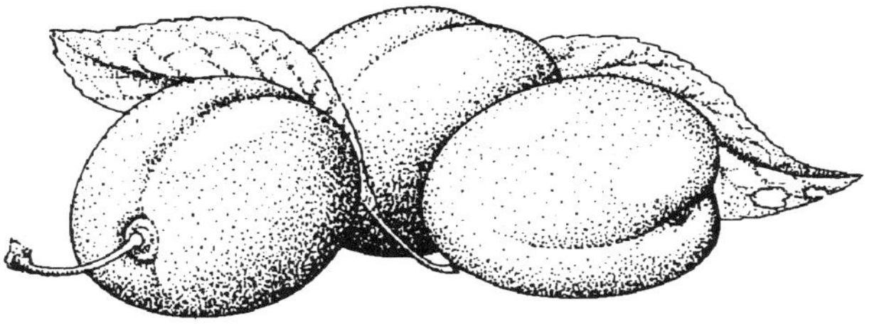

RIPE TOMATO SAUCE

Yield 3 litres (5 pints)

5 cm (2 inch) stick cinnamon
7 g (¼ oz) whole allspice
7 g (¼ oz) blade mace
600 ml (1 pint) distilled or white vinegar
5.5 kg (12 lb) fully ripe tomatoes
40 g (1½ oz) salt
pinch of cayenne pepper
7 g (¼ oz) paprika
500 g (1 lb) sugar
3 tbsp tarragon or chilli vinegar

1. Tie the whole spices loosely in a muslin bag, place in a pan with the distilled vinegar and bring slowly to the boil.
2. Remove from the heat, cover, and allow to infuse for 2 hours.
3. Wash and slice the tomatoes, place in a pan and cook until the skins are free. Rub the pulp through a sieve and return to a clean pan.
4. Add the salt, cayenne pepper, paprika, sugar and flavoured vinegar.
5. Cook to a creamy consistency.
6. Pour into warmed sauce bottles, cover and sterilise (page 71).

TOMATO AND PINEAPPLE RELISH

Yield 1.7 kg ($3^1/_2$ lb)

4 large cooking apples
525 g (1 lb 3 oz) can tomatoes
400 g (14 oz) can crushed pineapple
1.1 kg ($2^1/_2$ lb) sugar
$^1/_2$ tsp ground allspice
$^1/_2$ tsp ground cloves
$^1/_2$ tsp ground cinnamon
2 tsp Yorkshire relish or brown sauce
50 g (2 oz) salt
300 ml ($^1/_2$ pint) vinegar

1. Peel, core and chop the apples. Place all ingredients in saucepan, mix thoroughly. Bring to boil, simmer gently until mixture thickens, stirring occasionally.
2. Pour into warmed jars, cover and label.

WINTER RELISH

Yield 3 kg ($4^1/_2$ lb)

500 g (1 lb) cooking apples
375 g (12 oz) onions
1.5 kg (3 lb) blackberries
500 ml (1 pint) vinegar
1 tsp ground cinnamon
1 tsp ground allspice
15 g ($^1/_2$ oz) ground ginger
2 tbsp salt
6 cloves
6 peppercorns
500 g (1 lb) white sugar

1. Peel, core and chop the apples. Peel and chop the onions.
2. Place apples, onions and blackberries in a pan with the vinegar and spices, bring to the boil and simmer for 15–25 minutes.
3. Rub through a nylon sieve or a mouli-mill and return to a clean pan. Add the sugar, and stir until dissolved. Bring back to the boil and allow the mixture to boil rapidly until it thickens, approx. 20–30 minutes.
4. Pour into warmed jars, cover and label.

KEEPING MINT SAUCE

young mint, cleaned and chopped
vinegar
sugar
water

1. Fill a jar with mint. Cover with cold vinegar. Cover and store in a dark place.
2. When required, remove the desired amount and place in a sauceboat.
3. Add a little sugar; dilute with more vinegar and/or water.

Note: Sugar added to the stored sauce would cause fermentation.

STORE CUPBOARD ITEMS

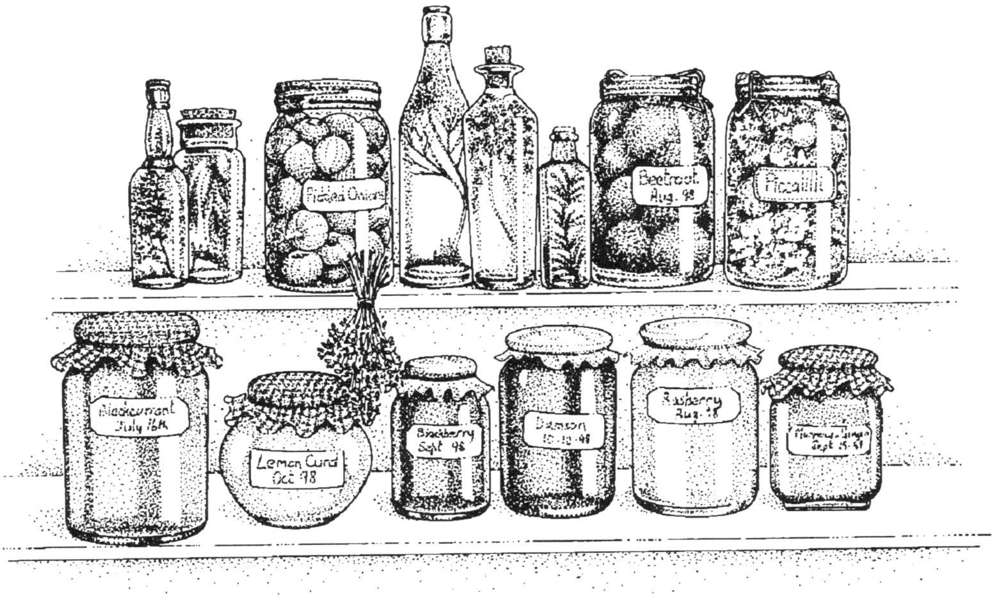

The recipes in this section are, strictly speaking, not preserves. All have their place in the store cupboard or the refrigerator; they are fun to make and add interest to dishes and menus and can replace commercial convenience products.

Curds contain eggs and butter in addition to the fruit and sugar, and are not intended to keep. As the temperature reached during cooking is low, curds should only be covered with a wax disc and cellophane cover.

Mincemeat, the traditional Christmas preserve, should be made at least two months in advance to allow flavours to develop and mature. The jar should be covered with a wax disc and cellophane cover and stored in a cool, dry place.

Oil is not a true preservative; it merely seals food. Foods stored in oil must be completely immersed, as should the flavouring agents in flavoured oils. Store in a cool, dry place or in the refrigerator.

APRICOTS OR PEACHES IN BRANDY

8 ripe apricots or peaches
110 g (4 oz) sugar
750 ml ($1^{1/2}$ pint) brandy

Blanch the fruit and peel. Slice or halve, removing centre of peaches with a teaspoon. Crack six stones and arrange the kernels in jars with the fruit. Add the sugar and brandy. Seal and leave for 4 weeks, shaking the jar daily.

Note:
The strength of alcohol can be reduced by diluting with sugar syrup (p. 77).

SUGAR SYRUP

110–250 g (4–8 oz) sugar
600 ml (1 pint) water

Dissolve sugar in the water. Bring to the boil. Boil for 2 minutes. Use as required.

CANDIED PEEL

citrus peel: oranges, lemons, limes, grapefruit, etc.
to 300 ml ($^{1/2}$ pint) liquid, add 175 g (6 oz) sugar

1. Scrub the fruit, cut in half and squeeze out the juice. Remove any remaining skin and flesh from the peel. Cut the peel into quarters.
2. Put peel in a saucepan and barely cover with water. Bring to boiling point and simmer until tender, approx. 1–2 hours.
3. Strain peel, measure liquid, add sugar. Dissolve sugar and return the peel to the syrup. Bring syrup to the boil. Allow sufficient syrup to cover the fruit.
4. Remove pan and leave to cool.
5. Day 2, bring the syrup and fruit to boiling point and simmer for 5 minutes. Leave to cool.
6. Day 3, bring to boiling point, simmer until syrup has been nearly absorbed.
7. Leave the peel on a cooling rack, on a sheet of greaseproof paper, pouring any spare syrup into the peel quarters.
8. Leave in a warm place.
9. Chop and use in cakes or cut in strips and dip in melted chocolate.

CUMBERLAND RUM BUTTER

450 g (1 lb) soft brown sugar
225 g (8 oz) butter
$^1/_2$ tsp ground nutmeg
2 tbsp rum

1. Ensure there are no lumps in the sugar by rolling between two sheets of greaseproof paper, or rubbing through a sieve. Place the sugar in a bowl.
2. Put the butter in a pan, heat gently until melted then heat until very hot but not disintegrating.
3. Pour the butter on to the sugar, add the nutmeg, and stir until the butter is fully incorporated.
4. Add the rum and stir again until well blended and a smooth texture.
5. Pour into an old-fashioned china bowl and allow to set.

FLAVOURED OIL

to 150 ml ($^1/_4$ pint) olive oil add:

either **2 cloves garlic, peeled, sliced and green centre removed**
or **25 g (1 oz) root ginger, peeled and sliced**
or **3–4 sliced fresh chillies** *or* **8 dried chillies**
or **a bunch of thyme**
or **a bunch of rosemary**
or **15 ml (1 tbsp) mixed wholespice**
or **the peeled zest of 1 lemon**
or **the peeled zest of 1 orange**

1. Place the flavouring in the oil and allow to infuse for 2 weeks before use.
2. Store in the refrigerator and use in French dressing, mayonnaise or to flavour soups, stews and stir fried food.

GOLDEN CURD

Yield 630 g ($1^1/_2$ lb)

50 g (2 oz) butter
2 oranges
or **zest of 1 and juice of 2 pink grapefruit**
225 g (8 oz) sugar
4 eggs (medium)
1 lemon

1. Place the butter in the top of a double saucepan, or in a bowl standing over a pan containing hot water, to melt.
2. Scrub the oranges and lemons and then finely grate the zest. Cut the fruit in half and squeeze out the juice. Add the rinds, juice and sugar to the butter and stir until sugar dissolves.
3. Beat the eggs and strain onto the fruit mixture. Cook gently, stirring occasionally, until the mixture thickens sufficiently to coat the back of the wooden spoon.
4. Pour into warmed jars, cover and label.

GOOSEBERRY CURD

Yield 1.8 kg (4 lb)

1.5 kg (3 lb) green gooseberries
600 ml (1 pint) water
750 g ($1^1/_2$ lb) sugar
150 g (4 oz) butter
4 eggs

1. Wash the gooseberries and place in a pan with the water. Simmer gently until tender, then sieve.
2. Place the sieved pulp in the top of a double saucepan, or in a bowl over a pan containing hot water. Add the sugar and stir until dissolved.
3. Add the butter. Beat the eggs well and strain on to the other ingredients. Stir well. Cook gently, stirring occasionally, until the mixture thickens sufficiently to coat the back of a wooden spoon.
4. Pour into warmed jars, cover and label.

HERB FLAVOURED VINEGAR

fresh herbs
cider or wine vinegar

Half-fill a wide-necked jar with freshly gathered leaves, picked just before flowering. Fill to the top with white vinegar and allow to steep for at least 14 days before use. The herbs may be left longer if desired.

LEMON CURD (1)

Yield 1.1 kg (2¼ lb)

4–5 lemons or 225 ml (8 fl oz) juice
175 g (6 oz) butter
550 g (1¼ lb) sugar
4 eggs or 225 ml (8 fl oz)

11..Wash fruit and finely grate zest from the lemons. Squeeze juice and use 225 ml (8 fl oz). Place butter, sugar, grated lemon zest and the juice in the top of a double saucepan, or in a bowl over a pan containing hot water. Cook gently until the sugar is dissolved. Strain and return to a clean pan or bowl.
2. Beat the eggs well, measure and strain on to the other ingredients. Return the pan to the heat and continue cooking over a low heat until the mixture thickens sufficiently to coat the back of a wooden spoon.
3. Pour into warmed jars, cover and label.

LEMON CURD (2)

Yield 300 g (10 oz)

150 g (5 oz) unsalted butter
225 g (8 oz) sugar
2 lemons
2 eggs

Follow method as for LEMON CURD (1) above.

MINCEMEAT (1)

Yield 3 kg (6 lb)

500 g (1 lb) cooking apples (prepared weight)
500 g (1 lb) currants
500 g (1 lb) seedless raisins
500 g (1 lb) sultanas
250 g (8 oz) chopped mixed peel
500 g (1 lb) suet, finely chopped or grated
500 g (1 lb) sugar, granulated or demerara
grated rind and juice of 2 lemons
50 g (2 oz) almonds, blanched and shredded
½ tsp mixed spice, or to taste
150 ml (¼ pint) whisky, rum or brandy (optional)

1. Mince apples, currants, raisins and sultanas coarsely. Mix all ingredients together (except the alcohol) and leave covered with a clean cloth or cling film at room temperature for three days, stirring two or three times daily.
2. Stir in the alcohol (if used) and pack the mincemeat into clean jars.
3. Cover with a wax disc and cellophane circle. Store in cool dry place.

Note: A firm, hard apple, eg. Wellington, is preferable to a Bramley seedling for good keeping.

MINCEMEAT (2)

Yield 800 g ($1^1/_2$ lb)

125 g (4 oz) Valencia raisins
125 g (4 oz) currants
125 g (4 oz) cooking apples, peeled
125 g (4 oz) demerara sugar
50 g (2 oz) sultanas
grated zest & juice of 1 lemon & 1 orange
50 g (2 oz) suet, finely chopped or grated
40 g ($1^1/_2$ oz) chopped mixed peel
25 g (1 oz) blanched almonds, grated
1 tbsp brandy
1 tbsp rum
1 tsp mixed spice

1. Mince together all the fruits except the currants.
2. Add all the remaining ingredients and stir well.
3. Pack into clean jars and cover with wax discs and cellophane circles.
4. Store in a cool dry place.

PICKLED LEMONS OR LIMES

3 lemons or limes
5 ml (1 tsp) salt
5 ml (1 tsp) paprika pepper
5 cloves
1 stick cinnamon
300 ml ($^1/_2$ pint) olive oil

1. Thinly slice lemons, lay on a wire rack and sprinkle with salt. Allow to dry for 24 hours in the kitchen (or 12 hours in a warm kitchen).
2. Layer in jam jars with paprika, cloves and cinnamon, and top with olive oil. Press down to ensure fruit is covered.
3. Label, "Use to flavour casseroles and stuffings".

SLOE GIN

1 kg (2 lb) ripe sloes
750 g ($1^1/_2$ lb) sugar
1.5 litres (3 pints) gin

1. Wipe the sloes and prick them all over with a needle. Half fill the preserving jars with them, sprinkle sugar on the fruit, pour the gin to fill the jars and seal tightly.
2. Leave for 12 weeks, shaking the jars occasionally.
3. Filter into attractive bottles. Store for at least one year.

Note: Damson or mulberry gin can be made in a similar way. There is no need to prick the mulberries.

SPILLIKINS

Syrup
112 g ($^{1}/_{4}$ lb) sugar
300 ml ($^{1}/_{2}$ pint) water

Spillikins
zest of 2 oranges or lemons peeled and thinly sliced

1. To make the syrup, dissolve the sugar in the water. Bring to the boil and simmer for 10 minutes.
2. Cook spillikins in boiling water until tender. Drain. Add to syrup, bring to boil, simmer for 5 minutes. Bottle in small 225 g ($^{1}/_{2}$ lb) jars. Cover and seal. Refrigerate after opening.

   Note: Use to decorate sweet dishes, eg. pancakes, or to garnish savoury dishes containing oranges or lemons.

RUMPOT

1 bottle light or dark rum
granulated sugar
strawberries, cherries, apricots, raspberries, plums, redcurrants, peaches, nectarines, grapes, melon
(Use a selection of fruit but avoid citrus fruit, and apples, bananas and pears)

1. The fruit must be sound, whole and ripe. It is possible to use just a few, choice fruits as they come into season. Use a special pot or a large stone crock.
2. Wipe the fruit gently. Do not peel or stone. Melon is the only fruit which should be peeled, seeded and cut into fairly large chunks. Put the fruit into the crock with its own weight of sugar and cover with rum.
3. Start rumpot with strawberries and cherries. Add fruit as it comes into season.
4. Keep completed rumpot for at least 3 months, tightly covered in a cool place.
5. Use the fruit and syrup in small quantities with ice-cream, cream or yoghurt.

MICROWAVE COOKING

Making preserves in the microwave is quicker than by conventional methods. Small batches can be made using fresh or frozen fruits.

Note:

1. Always use a cooking container three times larger than the ingredients to be used.
2. Use a wooden spoon for stirring the jams or preserves but do not leave the spoon in the oven whilst cooking.
3. Always follow the manufacturers instructions.
4. Cooking time varies with the wattage of the microwave.

BLACKBERRY JAM

450 g (1 lb) blackberries
juice of 1 small lemon
450 g (1 lb) sugar

1. Prepare the blackberries (if frozen, first defrost), and put into a 2.8 litre (5 pint) bowl with the lemon juice. Cook on HIGH for 10 minutes or until the fruit is soft and the volume of liquid is reduced.
2. Add the sugar and stir well. Cook on HIGH for 8–10 minutes, stirring every 5 minutes until setting point is reached.
3. Put into clean, warm jars. Seal with a twist top or a wax disc and with cellophane.

GOOSEBERRY JAM

Yield 675 g ($1\frac{1}{2}$ lb)

450 g (1 lb) gooseberries
200 ml ($\frac{1}{3}$ pint) water
450 g (1 lb) sugar

1. Prepare the gooseberries and put into a 2.8 litre (5 pint) bowl with the water. Cook on HIGH for 12 minutes or until the fruit is soft and the water reduced to approx. one-third quantity.
2. Add sugar and stir until dissolved.
3. Cook uncovered on HIGH for 9–10 minutes or until the setting point is reached.
4. Allow to cool slightly before potting in warmed jars. Seal.

LEMON CURD

2 lemons, zest and juice
2 eggs, whisked and sieved
110 g (4 oz) butter
225 g (8 oz) caster sugar

1. Place all the ingredients in a bowl. Heat on HIGH for one minute, then stir. Continue to cook for one minute bursts, stirring thoroughly in between each burst. Cook until the mixture has thickened, for approx. 5–8 minutes.
2. Pot and cover with a wax disc and cellophane. Store in refrigerator.

PLUM JAM

450 g (1 lb) plums
grated zest and juice of 1 small orange
$2\frac{1}{2}$ x 15 ml (1 tbsp) water
375 g (12 oz) granulated sugar

1. Halve and stone the plums, place in a large bowl with the water, orange zest and juice, and microwave for 8–10 minutes on HIGH until fruit is tender.
2. Add the sugar and stir until dissolved.
3. Cook on HIGH for 2 minutes. Stir.
4. Cook on HIGH for 8–10 minutes, stirring several times until setting point is reached.
5. Cool slightly before potting in warm jars.

RASPBERRY JAM

450 g (1 lb) frozen raspberries
450 g (1 lb) caster sugar

1. Place frozen raspberries in a 2 litre (4 pint) casserole. Microwave for 2–4 minutes on HIGH.
2. Stir in sugar until dissolved.
3. Microwave on HIGH until mixture achieves a rapid boil. Microwave on high to continue boiling for one minute.
4. Pour into warmed jars. Seal.

THREE FRUIT MARMALADE

Yield 1 kg (2 lb) yield

When marmalade supplies are running low, a small batch of the following recipe made in the microwave may fit the bill.

1 grapefruit
1 large lemon
1 orange
675 g (1½ lb) sugar
450 ml (¾ pint) boiling water

1. Scrub and pare the fruit and then shred finely. Place in a 2.9 litre (5 pint) bowl.
2. Squeeze out the juice and reserve.
3. Put the pith and pips in a piece of muslin and tie securely.
4. Put the muslin into the bowl with the zest shreds.
5. Pour 150 ml (¼ pint) boiling water onto the shreds, etc., and then leave for one hour.
6. Add the rest of the boiling water and the juice to the bowl.
7. Cook for 15 minutes on HIGH or until zest is tender. Allow to cool. Carefully squeeze the muslin bag.
8. Add the sugar and stir until dissolved. Cook for 20–25 minutes on HIGH, until setting point is reached.
9. Cool slightly before potting.

LOW SUGAR SPREADS

Low sugar spreads cannot be classed as 'preserves', because they do not contain enough sugar to prevent fermentation and to form a set. The sugar present in the recipes below is from the fruit and concentrated fruit juice.

In order to ensure the spread does not ferment, make in small quantities or freeze in ice-cube size amounts and thaw in the refrigerator for immediate use; or pour into small jars, cool and store in the refrigerator.

To set the spread, use gelatine, agar agar, or a proprietary gelling agent made from plant sources.

Can be made in the Microwave.

APRICOT MARMALADE

½ lemon
1 orange
110 g (4 oz) dried apricots
200 ml (⅓ pint) concentrated fruit juice
15 ml (3 tsp) agar agar

1. Scrub the orange and lemon. Peel and shred the peel thinly. Cook the peel in the juice until softened, approx. 1 hour.
2. Chop the fruit segments and apricots finely. Cook with the peel until tender.
3. Sprinkle the agar agar onto the mixture. Cook for a further 2 minutes.
4. Pour into freezer containers, chill and freeze.

BLACKCURRANT AND APPLE SPREAD *yield 450 g (1 lb)*

225 g (½ lb) apples, peeled and chopped
225 g (½ lb) blackcurrants, washed (juice)
200 ml (⅓ pint) concentrated apple juice
10 ml (2 tsp) lemon juice
15 ml (3 tsp) agar agar or gelatine

1. Cook the fruit with the juice and lemon juice until tender and mixture is thick.
2. Sprinkle the agar agar onto the fruit, stir thoroughly and boil for a further 2 minutes to ensure agar agar is completely dissolved.
3. To freeze, pour into small freezer containers. Cover with lids. Cool at room temperature. Chill in the refrigerator and freeze. To use, thaw in the refrigerator.

APRICOT AND APPLE SPREAD

350 g (3/4 lb) no-soak apricots
110 g (1/4 lb) apples
200 ml (1/3 pint) concentrated apricot juice
15 ml (1 tbsp) agar agar
juice and zest of 1/2 lemon
1/4 tsp cloves, ground

Use method as for BLACKCURRANT AND APPLE SPREAD above.

APRICOT AND PINEAPPLE SPREAD

225 g (1/2 lb) dried apricots
225 g (1/2 lb) pineapple, canned, crushed
200 ml (1/3 pint) concentrated fruit juice
1 tsp lemon juice
2 tsp sweet cicely stems, finely chopped
15 ml (3 tsp) agar agar

Use method as for BLACKCURRANT AND APPLE SPREAD above.

Note: Always use cooked or canned pineapple. Fresh pineapple contains an enzyme that destroys the setting property of gelatine.

CRANBERRY AND APPLE SPREAD

225 g (1/2 lb) cranberries
225 g (1/2 lb) apples
200 ml (1/3 pint) concentrated fruit juice
1/4 tsp allspice
1 tsp lemon juice
15 ml (3 tsp) agar agar

Use method as for BLACKCURRANT AND APPLE SPREAD above.

DATE AND APPLE SPREAD

350 g (3/4 lb) apples
110 g (1/4 lb) dates, chopped
150 ml (1/4 pint) water
1/4 tsp cinnamon or cloves
zest and juice of 1/2 lemon

Use method as for BLACKCURRANT AND APPLE SPREAD above.

INGREDIENTS INDEX

INGREDIENTS INDEX

INGREDIENTS INDEX

INGREDIENTS INDEX

INGREDIENTS INDEX

ABOUT THE WI

If you have enjoyed this book, the chances are that you would enjoy belonging to the largest women's organisation in the country – the National Federation of Women's Institutes, or the WI as it is usually known.

We are friendly, go-ahead, like-minded women, who derive enormous satisfaction from all the movement has to offer. The list is long – you can make new friends, have fun and companionship, visit new places, develop new skills, take part in community services, fight local campaigns, become a WI Market producer, and play an active rôle in an organisation which has a national voice.

The WI is the only women's organisation in the country that owns an adult education establishment. At Denman College, you can take a course in anything from car maintenance to paper sculpture, from book binding to yoga, or cordon bleu cookery to fly fishing.

For more information about the WI, write to the **National Federation of Women's Institutes, 104 New Kings Road, London SW6 4LY or telephone 0171-371-9300. The NFWI Wales Office is at 19 Cathedral Road, Cardiff CF1 9LJ, telephone 01222-221712.**

ABOUT THE AUTHOR

Pat Hesketh, a trained home economics teacher, has enjoyed a long career teaching and advising in cookery and crafts in schools, further education and adult education. During ten years as Home Economics Adviser to the National Federation of Women's Institutes, she acted as consultant on several published craft and cookery books, and travelled extensively lecturing and tutoring WI members in all aspects of home economics and crafts. She now runs a small guest house in the heart of the Yorkshire Dales, but still finds time to be active in the WI locally, helps tutor courses for her county federation and the National Federation, and occasionally tutors at Denman College.

SILVER SPOON
THE FINE ART OF PRESERVING

Silver Spoon is Britain's number one sugar company. They supply more than half the nation's total sugar requirements. They also have the largest range and have an excellent track record in developing new and interesting sugar products. The area of preserving is no exception to this; there is a **Silver Spoon** sugar product for making all types of jams, jellies and marmalades.

Silver Spoon Preserving Sugar has been specially developed for making jams and jellies with fruits that are naturally high in pectin, such as Seville oranges, plums, gooseberries and blackcurrants. The large sugar crystals dissolve more slowly, preventing a heavy layer of sugar settling on the bottom of the pan, which means that less stirring is required and this results in a clearer, brighter jam. **Preserving Sugar** also produces hardly any froth, which cuts down on the amount of skimming.

The pectin content of many fruits, particularly soft fruits such as strawberries, raspberries and loganberries, is very low, so **Silver Spoon** have developed a sugar particularly for these fruits. **Jam Sugar** has been specially formulated to contain the correct amount of natural apple pectin that will ensure a jam or jelly sets quickly and successfully. This sugar only requires a 4 minute boil, which is an added advantage and speeds up the jam making process for a fresher, fruitier jam.

For those who wish to add pectin to sugar separately, **Silver Spoon** have developed a natural citrus pectin in powder form which is available in a carton of 3 easy-to-use sachets. One 13g sachet of **Silver Spoon Pectin** is the correct amount to use with 1 kg of **Silver Spoon Granulated Sugar** and is an essential ingredient to help soft fruit jams and jellies set successfully. The pectin is sprinkled over the fruit with the sugar and stirred until completely dissolved, before boiling. Again, this product only requires a 4 minute boil, which results in a fresher, fruitier flavour and a brighter, clearer colour.

All **Silver Spoon** products have full instructions and recipe ideas printed on the pack, but for more recipes contact the **Silver Spoon Creative Kitchen, The Silver Spoon Company, British Sugar plc, Oundle Road, Peterborough, PE2 9QU**.

MORE WI BOOKS TITLES

WI Books is a publishing company wholly owned by the National Federation of Women's Institutes to publish and make available books of good value and special interest to WI members. There are many titles on Cooking, Crafts and Gardening, Painting and Drawing; there are also Quiz Books, a history of the WI, and of Denman College, a nostalgic book of autographs and some children's books. A catalogue is available from WI Books Ltd, Glebe House, Church Street, Crediton, Devon EX17 2AF. 1998 prices are shown for the following cookery titles selected from the list, and written by WI members:

The WI Book of Bread and Bakes *by Kay Bradley* £4.95
Written especially for WI members, with intriguing new recipes for experienced cooks and encouragement for those who are not quite sure where to start.

The WI Book of Cooking for One *by Margaret Foss* £4.95
Makes 'cooking for one' delicious, easy and interesting, as well as healthy, with suggestions for a basic store cupboard and kitchen equipment.

Other titles available in the original, highly popular *WI Book of* ... cookery series, with recipes tried and tested by the WI.

Biscuits	£3.95	**Pastry**	£1.80
Cakes	£2.95	**Soups and Starters**	£2.95
Fish and Seafood	£2.95	**Vegetables and Salads**	£2.95
Microwave Cookery	£2.95		

A Taste of WI Markets £4.95
More than 135 recipes celebrate WI Markets' outstanding reputation as a source of fresh homemade cooking.

The Family Vegetarian *by Mary Norwak* £4.95
An extensive variety of delicious non-meat dishes with nutrition advice. For the family who want vegetarian meals within everyday cooking.

Simply Good Food *by NFWI Wales* £4.95
Over 130 recipes to make you feel well, look well and be well, using foods low in fat, salt and sugar, and high in fibre, to produce delicious and healthy food.